52 Reasons to Live

Why Greatness Refuses to Die

Gessy Martinez, LPC, LCDC, NCC

Aspire and Reach for More, LLC
Austin, Texas

Copyright page

This book has been written to provide helpful information on the subjects discussed, and is not meant to be used to diagnose or treat any medical or mental health condition. For diagnosis or treatment of any medical problem, consult your own medical or mental health professional. The publisher and author aren't responsible for any condition that may require medical supervision. They're not liable for any damages or negative consequences from any treatment, action, application, or preparation to any person reading or following the information in this book.

Neither the publisher nor the individual author(s) shall be liable for any physical, psychological, emotional, financial, or commercial damages, including but not limited to special, incidental, consequential, or other damages. Resources are provided for informational purposes only and do not constitute an endorsement of any websites or resources. Readers should be aware that the websites and resource contact information listed in this book may change.

Although I'm a licensed professional counselor, I'm not your counselor. Reading this book doesn't create a patient-client relationship between us. This book shouldn't be used as a substitute for the mental health services of a competent mental health professional, credentialed and authorized to practice in your state or country.

Contents

Welcome Greatness ☺

I wrote this book with you in mind. I was thinking about the ways I could encourage you to view your life and circumstances differently. Suppose we had a conversation about some of the thoughts that you were having, and the feelings that caused you to be discouraged. I wrote this book thinking about how I could say something to help you understand, to see yourself with eyes of love and compassion.

This book was written to help you look beyond mistakes, beyond failures, and to see beyond what other people have said about you. To see yourself as someone entirely worthy of living a beautiful life, someone who is fully capable and deserves a wonderful life experience. I want you to see a hopeful future and see your potential, to imagine the life you were born to live.

Change is a prolonged process. It's one of the hardest things for human beings to understand. It's difficult to wait for change and sit through the process, because we want to know "how does it end?" We want someone to tell us, "It's going to be good." We want promises: "Promise me that it's going to be good. Promise me that I'm going to get what I want."

We want to hear "Promise me that it's not going to be painful," or "Tell me it's not embarrassing, or not what I imagined." "Promise me that it won't take work, time, effort, or sacrifice."

When we don't hear the right kind of promises made, when we can't see the end, we get scared. We make excuses, and find reasons to support the negative beliefs. We then start to debate in our minds, finding reasons why we shouldn't go on, or why we shouldn't believe the best.

Finding reasons why we shouldn't hope. Sometimes we work harder at looking for all the reasons why we can't change. The idea of giving up the known pain for the unknown possibilities causes us to search for reasons that go against hope. Repeated effort and energy go into thinking about ways to prove ourselves right, and ways to believe the negative, rather than possibilities. Although desperately wanting to think the best, we allow thoughts of the worst-case scenario or the impossible to consume us — for example, "It's never going to happen," or "Good things only happen to other people." If you allow these thoughts to persist, they'll get louder and louder. You'll start to believe they're right when they're not. Everyone wants to have hope; some people have to fight harder than others to see the dream become reality.

Everybody wants to believe the best, but for some, it's not just an empty belief. You have to work at building hope, fighting mentally against every disbelief and false idea that repeatedly comes along, until the hope is more substantial — and louder — than the doubt. For some, the battle in the mind feels like an ongoing, long-lasting war, a continuous fight where you fall down, and bouncing back up is difficult, while for other people, it's an occasional thought, equal to one fight, and they get back up right away. They use the time between rounds to catch their breath. The thoughts come back, the struggle continues, and the will to fight requires more and more from you each time.

Don't give up just because the desire to keep fighting may seem to take more out of you than you want to give. While it may feel like you're losing, the truth is you're winning. You're building every day on the fact that today I rise, today I fight, and today I win. Keep moving forward, keep going, and each time you take those small steps, you're telling the enemy in your mind, "Not today, not me, not this time." You're also sending this message to yourself: "I'm in this fight to Win It!"

If you've experienced thoughts of suicide, if you're concerned about a loved one who's attempted suicide in the past or is currently having suicidal thoughts, this book was designed to help you think of reasons to live, enjoy, and thrive in life. After reading this book, don't stop with just the reasons you've noted. Add your own reasons, and move in the direction of your goals and dreams. Make the reasons a source of joy.

If you've lost someone to suicide in the past, if you've dealt with the loss of a loved one, or have known of a suicide attempt by someone at work or school, you're the reason I've written this book: to make a difference and build hope in others and inspire them to *live*.

1
This is just the beginning of your Hero's Journey

In his book *The Hero's Journey,* Joseph Campbell writes that all heroes make a decision to move on. There are steps or moments in their life where the hero decides to move from their old life to a new life. Consider the problem you're facing right now as your moment of decision. The beginning is where you have a chance to choose to move your life forward or remain the same. If you decide to move forward, to keep living, then you're taking a positive step to create change in your life.

Your choice to live another day means saying "Yes" to becoming the hero of your story. I hope your curiosity is piqued right now. What if you become the hero? What if everything that you're facing is here to show your mental and emotional strength? What if what you're dealing with is here to make you stronger emotionally, not to break you?

Like most heroes, you'll face tests, allies, and enemies. The tests are challenges to help you build resiliency or highlight an area in your life that needs change or improvement. Use the stress to grow emotional muscles, rather than let it weigh you down. Push back against it and use its weight for your benefit. Like weights in a gym, there are times when the weights are heavy, but you can build the strength to bear more over time. We need to let someone else be a coach or a spotter for the heavier weights.

During the hero's journey, there's a time when a wise

mentor comes along to help guide the hero and reveal to them their potential. The mentor comes to help speak the truth to the hero, showing them they have what it takes to make it — for instance, getting professional help if the feeling of giving up is building or suicidal thoughts are growing. Your therapist is your spotter, helping to teach you the proper form for handling your thoughts and learning how to bear the weight in a way that works to give you strength.

2

You're still here, so you've already won

Every day that you continue to live is a choice you're making to win. You can't lose when you're moving forward.

Every day is a new chance and a new opportunity. Just getting up and choosing to stay in the fight is a winning move. You've already won by simply opening your eyes this morning and starting over.

Choose the winning side of life by taking small, consistent steps. You win by waking up.

You win by winning the morning, getting out of bed, and getting dressed.

You win when you don't make excuses.

You win by having courage.

You win when you choose to believe, and to be hopeful about tomorrow.

You win when you ask for help.

You win when, even in the face of uncertain odds that may seem to be stacked against you, you choose to believe that you can win.

You win by deciding to live, not die.

You win by deciding to try, instead of giving up.

You win when you forgive yourself.

You win when you extend kindness to yourself and others.

You win when you keep reaching for your goals, even after a failure.

You win when you free yourself from unfair expectations.

You win when you try, over and over again, until change occurs.

You win when you give yourself options.

You win when you commit to change and to grow.

You win by having the courage to take the next step, and come out of the cave you may find yourself hiding in.

You win by making the bed and telling yourself, "I won't go back to bed," because what was once a place of comfort is becoming your sick bed. It's becoming a bed that's holding you down, rather than propping you up. You win when instead of using the bed as a shield, you make a decision to carry your weight and bear your burden.

Deciding how you'll use your time is another free choice you're making. Don't spend time rehearsing all the things you think you've done wrong. Don't hit the replay button on the "greatest hits of my failures or disappointments." Don't turn on the stereo that plays the tracks of fear over and over. Play over in your mind that you're *still here*, which makes you victorious over yesterday. You've defeated the temptation to give up, each time you stay in the game of life.

3
Your family doesn't need perfect — they need you

You'll never be perfect, and the world isn't looking for perfect; it's your imperfection that invites others into your life. There are times where we avoid someone or put off doing something because we want thing to be perfect. We think that we can't give or do perfectly, and so we avoid until we believe we can.

Not everyone or everything deserves your energy, but your family needs and deserves it — including all of your imperfections. Think of imperfections like puzzle pieces: if all of them were the same shapes, they wouldn't fit together to make a complete picture. Without the different shapes, the pieces can't blend and make room to come together. Each puzzle piece may not appear to have the "right" shape looking at it alone, but the right body makes room for the next part to fit. The goal is to adjust and add until a beautiful picture is revealed.

Perfection leaves no room to grow, nor does it give others the ability to add to your life. *Imperfect* has room to change, grow, and allows others to add to your life. Your family never asked for perfect — and if someone did, they were mistaken, because perfect doesn't exist. If someone were perfect, they wouldn't exist here on Earth. Excellence is a goal that can be reached, but not maintained — because it's merely someone's opinion or judgment as to whether that state has been met. Love never requires perfection; it's imperfection that makes love possible, and love has room for others to come and lend a hand or add to your life.

When someone is willing enough to be vulnerable and allow their imperfection to show, that opens the door for connection. Your relationships need displays of empathy and grace; it's very natural to be imperfect, and powerful to allow others permission to be flawed.

4
You're valuable and worthy of a good life

Other people don't determine your value or worth. Whether or not someone is happy with you doesn't lessen or change how important you're as a person. You're valuable. You are worthy of a good life.

Your worth isn't tied to your actions, your family, or how others think of you. It isn't dependent on how you feel about yourself. Behavior and actions have consequences, but never taking one's life. **Life isn't a price for behavior.**

You're priceless. Low self-esteem isn't an indicator of your worth. Having value doesn't mean being flawless: having value means you'll have flaws and make mistakes. The mistakes don't define you. Other people don't define you.

Self-respect is necessary, but if you feel ashamed or have done something that feels shameful, that's *not* an indicator of your worth as a human being. If you've made poor choices or misbehaved, that *doesn't* make you a "bad" person. Taking responsibility is necessary for change, but don't confuse responsibility with punishment. You may not feel terrific about yourself, but how you think of yourself doesn't make you any less worthy than you truly are.

Your life has the same value and respect as that of the person next to you. You have the same ability for redemption as someone who has behaved well in the eyes of others. You're worthy of forgiveness, and you can start over.

Sometimes it takes a significant event to get our attention and to force us to decide.

That decision isn't, "Should I live or not?" The choice you have to make is, "Which road will I take from here? Will I go back to my old life, or move forward and change?" You'll not always necessarily want the change, or think you need it. Change comes without warning, in the form of a relationship failing, a mistake with terrible consequences, or a business or opportunity falling apart. It's not convenient or comfortable.

What looks like the end can be the beginning of your new start, but you won't know the possibilities unless you decide to give change a try. Who said you're not valuable or worthy? Who has the right to determine this in your life?

Only the maker of a thing can place a price or value on it. Your life is too high a price for you to pay, and infinitely too high a way to discount your worth. You're not an accident of creation. There was a purpose when you were born. It doesn't matter how your parents met or the story behind your conception. What's important is that you possess enormous value, whether or not you feel like you do.

5
Forgiveness is possible

"I have hurt people …"

You can be forgiven. You can make up for the hurt and learn to forgive yourself. Even if someone you've hurt doesn't want to have anything to do with you, you can help others who've been hurt. Similarly, you can teach others how not to get damaged the same way. You can tell the truth and prevent future pain and suffering. Sometimes the best person to advise someone what *not* to do is a person who's done it, had a negative outcome, and now feels the impact of their decisions on others. A simple example of this would be a bully who has realized the effect their behaviors and words had on others, and now advocates for others and teaches young people how to deal with or fight against bullying.

Know what you're capable of, because after you've done the healing work to get better, you're changed — and can help other people who've struggled with the same issues.

Sometimes we do things that surprise ourselves. We may behave in a way we never thought possible, doing things we don't like or want to be done to us, instead of punishing ourselves by doing something as final as suicide. We can seek professional help and learn how to give and receive forgiveness so that we can release and heal from the emotional pain.

Stay alive to receive forgiveness, to be an agent of healing where you once were an agent of pain. You can help others repair their lives just by staying alive, allowing and helping them to forgive, and allowing yourself to be forgiven. Forgiving others and letting go of bitterness and pain can free you to enjoy life. Your mental, emotional, and physical health can improve with the act of forgiveness.

Receiving forgiveness from those we've hurt can be the first step to healing those relationships. Your mental health will improve when the feelings of guilt and shame are gone. For some people, their symptoms of depression are lessened, or even disappear altogether, when they receive and give forgiveness from and to others. Asking someone else for forgiveness opens up the door to empathy. Maybe the other person was unaware of your struggle, or what you thought when the incident happened. Seeking forgiveness may be a way to share your story and your truth and receive empathy. It humanizes the offender. This isn't guaranteed, but you can gain emotionally just by attempting it.

Causing someone you love pain can be heartbreaking, devastating, and leave you not wanting to face them — or anyone. When we go against our values, or how we see ourselves, we disappoint ourselves and can be left questioning what we believe. Forgiving yourself after failing repeatedly becomes more difficult each time. The first step is accepting that you're human and will make mistakes, some significant failures or choices and others less so.

No one gets through life without committing errors and experiencing failures. It's part of living. By making changes and aligning what you believe with what you do — that's, your values with your actions — you can change the number of mistakes you make, and prevent life-altering, painful errors.

If you take the lessons you learn and apply them permanently, your mistakes can lead to growth and maturity, making them a part of your new belief system. Resolve that next time, you're going to handle whatever led to the error or failure differently. Have a plan in place to help you when the temptation comes to do the same thing again. Forgive yourself completely; don't try to forgive yourself, only to allow yourself to perseverate on negative thoughts. Forgive yourself, seek forgiveness from others when appropriate, and remind yourself, "I'm forgiven" when those thoughts come.

See the hope that can come from receiving forgiveness. Take your focus off the fear and the shame, and believe you can get better, heal, and prevent this from happening again. The feelings you have can pass, and the dark cloud that has followed you can dissipate. It will take courage, loving yourself enough to forgive yourself, and believing you're worthy of forgiveness. Your very willingness to read this and believe it's possible shows that inside you lies the ability to do good. Start doing good by forgiving yourself, and releasing yourself from the prison you've walked into in your mind and heart.

6

Prove the negative people wrong

The negative voices in your head are lying. Don't listen to the message that tries to oppress or depress you. While you may hear it, remember you don't have to *accept* it. Reject the negative message each time it comes, like the proverbial hot potato. You can catch it like a ball in your hand, but if you hold on to it long enough, it becomes dangerous. Your heart and mind see the negative thoughts as a bomb, meant to blow up your dreams, desire and hope. Don't catch or keep negativity. Don't hold it. Don't receive it. You can refuse to catch it.

Prove the negative people wrong. Choose not to receive harmful feedback, and make up your mind not to believe accusations and destructive ideas. Don't let doubt form. Do your best, and don't quit! Your haters are waiting and expecting you to stop. Don't give up on yourself or your life. People won't always understand or support your goals. Whether or not their actions are malicious doesn't matter. Believe in yourself.

Human beings are by nature selfish and have to work against the instinct to be selfish every day. We have to work at being intentionally generous or kind. Set your mind on success and your motives to be positive. Be successful by keeping promises to yourself and your loved ones. Proving the accusers or negative people in your life wrong will be a by-product of achieving success for yourself.

Let the haters go by, not allowing their words or actions to take over the thoughts in your mind. Don't waste your energy trying to make your enemies into friends or fans. Unless they come to you'llingly, you have more to lose than gain trying to win them over.

Why would someone be purposely hostile toward you when you haven't done anything to them? It can be due to a range of emotions like jealousy, fear, feelings of being competitive, or just plain ignorance. Some people don't know how to relate to others; this inability to connect can be interpreted as unsupportive. However, they may just lack empathy, concern, or people or communication skills.

Sometimes we make the mistake of spending our energy trying to prove someone wrong. Then, when we reach a goal or accomplish what we set out to achieve, we can become discouraged if that person doesn't validate our accomplishment. If we do this, we may feel worse off than when we started. The best way to prove your haters wrong is with the right attitude: to be motivated from inside yourself. That way, no matter the outcome, you enjoy the progress and success you've achieved because you don't need your haters to approve or support you in order to be proud of yourself!

Proving them wrong is an attitude in your heart; it's like going to the gym and working out twice a day and never letting anyone know that you're doing it. They'll see the results as your body shape changes, and as your mental health improves.

When you put time and energy into any goal, the results will show. You can be successful starting in secret, and later others will see the results. Someone who goes to the gym and works out regularly can't hide it, because after a while their improved health will be obvious to anyone who can see.

7

You have a unique gift, way of being, and awareness of what the world needs

Decide that your version of the world has value. Your unique perspective doesn't have to conflict with the world. Your uniqueness can coexist with the world around you and add depth, beauty, and hope to others. Your unique perspective can help others release and engage in their uniqueness.

You have a unique gift, way of being, and awareness of what the world needs. How can you be unique when everyone is the same? For an example, more than 1,000 genres and styles of music exist in the world. There's no other sound like your sound. No way of seeing and being in the world like you do. Even if you try to imitate someone, you'll never duplicate them because you're an original.

Becoming at peace with who you're, and happy with everything about yourself, takes time and practice. Practice sharing your gift with others, whether it's helping others, listening to them, or showing compassion. Make a list of your strengths and set out to use your gifts to help others. Help brighten someone's day and help them to accomplish something that will help improve their life. If you want to figure out what your strengths are, try answering the following questions:

What are some of the good things people say about you?

Are you a good listener or problem-solver?

What do you advise others about?

What are you known among your friends for?

Growing up, how did others describe your personality?

When have you been successful in the past? What skills helped you survive a terrible situation in the past?

If you're trying to figure out your strengths and gifts, try answering the following questions:

What can I do well?

What are others asking me to help with all the time?

What's something I do well that seems to come effortlessly to me?

What hobbies do I like?

What's something I enjoyed doing as a kid?

What's one thing I love to do, and time gets lost when I'm doing it?

What's something others have said I'm a natural at doing?

Your personality and talents occupy a unique space in the world. You're made up of a unique DNA, perspective, and way of looking at the world. You live and interpret the world in a way no one else can because of your uniqueness. Embrace the difference and see the beauty and the joy that can come from being different, not the same.

8

There's a job, a mission, and a role that only you can fulfill

There's a job, a mission, and a role that only you can fulfill. No one else can do the job, deliver the product, say the words, or touch another life the way you can. You fill three essential aspects: working a job, having a mission, and filling a role. Let's clarify some definitions going forward.

Job: a task or piece of work that you're paid or compensated for performing or completing.

Mission: what you were born to do, how you'll impact the world or community.

Role: a description of your position based on responsibility and/or relationship to others.

There's a reason you're not happy right now with your job or your position. Some of the restlessness or disappointment you've felt related to work may signify that it's time to do something different. Look at creating or finding your calling as a way to get more out of both work and life.

<u>You start by asking questions like:</u>
What do I get excited talking about, and could speak forever about?

What makes me happy when I'm doing it?

What's something I've done in the past that's given me the greatest satisfaction?

What are the things I value in my life?

What issues am I passionate about defending?

What would I choose if there were something in this world that I could change, get rid of, or add?

There's a unique position, a unique calling that only you can fulfill. Everything about you — your experiences, likes, and handicaps — is useful in talking, encouraging, and helping others like yourself. Your uniqueness can help another person in a tough time in their lives. Everyone needs connections. This is how we learn about ourselves, by interacting with others. You have something that others want to connect with, and it's how you're different that makes you unique and rare.

You may view some traits as negative, not valuable or insignificant — but someone who doesn't make music might think a talent for playing multiple instruments is something to be admired. They might look at such a person as a teacher who can show them how to play. Some people will pay to learn to something that you do naturally, or don't take very seriously. For example, what if a tall person meets a teenager struggling with self-esteem issues because of their height and spends some time encouraging the young person, assuring them that their height won't be an issue but an asset one day?

Your characteristics can be opportunities to find purpose. The unique qualities you possess can become part of your mission or calling, and you can use them to help others with similar backgrounds.

These parts of who you are can be used to do something which allows you to express yourself and connect with others trying to do the same thing.

If you take the time to think about what you enjoy and get excited about, you'll find some clues as to your calling. Think about what you love to do: if time or money weren't factors, you'd do it all the time. The calling in your life and the unique role you play in society has been set in your heart and mind from when you were young. Some of it has been drowned out by life through other people's opinions about what you "should" do. Some of these voices have been hiding in their own fear or self-doubt, unable to visualize anyone like you doing the thing you dream of doing.

Your calling is a pull, a restlessness in your heart and mind to do something — but you may not always know how to do it. It will pull you in the direction in which you're supposed to go. But what happens with those who don't live out their purpose or calling? The restlessness stays, and they miss out on enjoying the best part of life: seeing the best of who they're expressed, and giving back to the world in their unique and memorable way. Don't let fear, worry or doubt block out the dream in your heart. Those cares, worries, concerns, and self-defeating thoughts will send you in the opposite direction of your calling.

9

Just by being born you've made a difference and changed everyone's roles

The moment you were created, you mattered. The months and days leading to your birth and the day of your birth — you mattered! You've changed the lives of others from the day you were conceived. Anna Vital, author and founder of Adioma, did the math: "On average, we live for 78.3 years. Most of us remember people we meet after age five. Assuming we interact with three new people daily, 365 days a year plus leap years days is 365.24. In total it will be $(78.3 - 5) \times 3 \times 365.24 = 80{,}000$ people."

What would you say to 80,000 people? How could you leave a positive mark in their lives? Even if you start late and only impact 50,000 people, your life still has potential. One life affects the story of another. Your mother became a mother because of you. Even if you were child number two, three, or four, you're the reason she can claim being the mother of two, three, or four, and that will never change. Your father became a father because of you; you're the reason that his role exists. Your family tree added a name when you were born.

Your family tree added a branch with your name. Your unique personality and story began when you were born, and continued to play out. Even if you're the only bright fruit on your family tree, inside of you is potential. Even at 30, 40, 50, or 60 years old, there remains potential. Don't end the possibilities for a turnaround.

You could be the defining force in your family: the turnaround, the hope, and the dream of your family name standing for something amazing.

When you were born, your family imagined a new future with you in it, and they made room and a place just for you. They correctly believed that you'd be a part of how their lives would change forever.

No one imagines the end of that life, just the addition to the family. You not being a part of the family was never planned; this is one reason why the death of a loved one is traumatic. Your parents believed the best when they met you. Even if you weren't raised with your parents or by them, inside you was their aspiration — even if life, disease, addiction, or selfishness took them away from you. Parents have hopes and dreams for their children. For some, it's life stressors, addiction, and trauma that stop them from sharing, or helping the process. Despite this, you matter, and you have a purpose that can change things not just for you but your family, too.

10

By living, you add to the meaning of family and friends' lives; by dying, you take away from it

Hearts will break, lives will change, and the story of your loved ones will never be the same. The loss will become the only thing that some of your loved ones know or talk about when you're gone.

When I take a step back and think about people who have come into my life, either for long periods or very short moments, it makes me happy. I'm surprised by the impact that strangers and the love of friends can have on my life. I've had some simple moments on a train or airplane with a talkative stranger. I've exchanged laughter and smiles with children. I've walked and helped an older adult. I've helped a stranger find direction, given money to a homeless person, and stood up for someone in a store.

Let's look at the ways you may have helped someone in the past:

— Said something kind to a stranger who was looking kind of down.

— Held a friend's hand in a hospital.

— Helped a friend through an embarrassing moment.

— Spent time with a stranger in a stuck elevator and laughed about it.

— Helped a friend move to a new place.

— Cleaned or helped build the house of a stranger.

- Looked for a lost animal.
- Found a phone and gave it back to the owner.
- Held a package for your neighbor.
- Gave a tip to a waiter or waitress with a thank you.
- Told someone in your life how much they mean to you.
- Were there when a friend was in crisis.
- Gave a hug to someone who was crying.
- Helped a customer in a time of confusion and a stranger in a time of crisis.

Life is full of small and big moments where we add to the lives of others. These are moments when you were needed. These moments are points where we connect with others. The most significant impact you can make in someone else's life is just being there; it's not about having the right words or something smart to say, it's just your presence. It's about not being alone when you need someone and having a shoulder to lean on when life gets heavy.

Connecting with others out of compassion, frustration, fear, hope, or just sharing a laugh are all points of connection. You've had many relationships in your life; think back to the small ones with neighbors or strangers as well as the significant relationships with loved ones, teachers, mentors, and those who have shown you love and kindness.

We only get one chance to live this life, so why not get the most out of it by enjoying both the little things and the big moments? Life is full of sweet possibilities buried in the tough days. Look for them, and pull out of life all the small sweet stuff it has to offer.

11
Every life has something to offer

By leaving too soon, your unique beauty will be missing from the world. Look at one life that had something to offer in a short time: a child who lived a day or a week. That week the child lived had something to offer because that child stopped time and changed lives of its parents when they were born. That child wrapped the hopes and dreams of its parents.

Whether young or old, children always needs to belong, to feel connected, and to be reminded that someone out there loves them and cares about them. It's not how much money you make as a parent; it's not about how perfect you are; it's about your ability to love them and show them that they're worthy of love.

Your life brought something into the world, and the people in your life needed you. You have something to offer to the people around you. You have something to provide to your co-workers, fellow students, and the people in your family. They may not understand or even acknowledge this fact, but it's true. Every life has something to offer; just because you're feeling down or may need more than you can give right now doesn't mean that you don't have something to give.

Many times, we place value on the wrong things in life. The lasting and beneficial things don't come with price tags on them. What's most valuable to others are the things you can't always see, feel, taste, or touch. These are gifts that people give from the heart to one another which become a part of their relationship, a part of their story of friendship, brotherhood, or sisterhood. It's what connects them; it helps to make a memory or leave a positive mark on the heart or emotions.

Your life is valuable. This is why, when a life is taken by violence or accidently, there is a price to pay and laws to uphold the sanctity of life. This is why those who are religious, realize their life is invaluable because it was brought by God. Your life has an incredible value, whether you apply the laws of spirituality or the laws of justice.

Begin by believing your life has value. Then, move forward by treating yourself with the dignity your life deserves by not harming yourself. Love yourself with the love you deserve by finding the courage to keep going and to keep moving forward. Honor yourself by committing not to harm yourself or others.

You have something to offer. Imagine doing the following:

1) Open up your arms and let someone in.

2) Reach down your arm and pull someone up. Repeat as often as needed, and more often when feeling sad.

See yourself as having something to offer to others.

12
Everything can be repaired or made new from the broken pieces

The thing that you were trying to hide, run from or forget will change. Broken things can be fixed when the right adhesive is added; anything can be repaired. You may be responsible for breaking up the pieces of your life by a decision you made, or because of an addiction. You can also be accountable and be a part of actively repairing your life. I want to encourage you to believe that your relationships can be restored.

Living past your feelings, staying in the game and adventure of life gives you the time to see this happen. Strength and courage are needed to repair broken relationships. Your addiction may have resulted in the loss of marriage, money, job, self-respect, relationships, dignity, and hope. But all this is reparable, and the broken pieces can either be put back together or used to make something new and stronger. Without you, things can't be fixed completely. This is why you have to hold on and stay in the fight: to recover what was lost and repair what's broken.

Let's start with some of the things that you can repair:
— The lies can be fixed by telling the truth behind why you did what you did.
— Communicate with loved ones to let them know what you're dealing with emotionally right now.

Rebuilding trust requires consistent action and keeping your promises, one commitment followed through at a time.

Your family may need to hear the story with the help of counseling and boundaries to help protect them from unnecessary pain.

It will be difficult to face those you've hurt, but telling the truth can help you and others to heal. It will allow space in their heart that's been filled with lies, cover-ups, and conflict to heal. It can also bring to light other vital issues.

The healing process is like helping a friend clean his apartment. Before you can start to clean the apartment, you have to turn on the lights and assess what's there and how much of a mess is in the room. Does it need a complete overhaul, or only minor repairs? Is there layer upon layer of mess, or does it look clean until you start to touch stuff in the apartment and realize it's been crumbling for years? It can be repaired; the room can be clean, fortified, and made new. The healing process is about looking at the problem, addressing it, and using tools and skills to help clean and make things new and functional again.

Some family members will stay and go in with you, and some will be relieved if they can leave the room. You can begin the work of making repairs on your own because they had to bear the burden for too long. Some loved ones will be hiding in a corner, while others will be standing in the middle of the room with boxing gloves on.

Someone will have ideas about how to clean the room, and watch you every step of the way; they might become your stumbling block, but stick with it. Your life — like this room — can be cleaned up; it can all be repaired and made new.

Set realistic expectations going forward. This isn't intended to make you think that your life will instantly become better; you'll need the help of a professional to learn new ways to cope and live. This process can take a long time, and will happen quickly in some relationships and may take years in others. You'll need help repairing the bonds and dealing with some things not turning out the way you wanted or expected. Repair does't necessarily mean that you get what you want, but the goal is to start the healing process, and to ask for and receive forgiveness.

It's important to remember that repairing one relationship may mean letting go of another. For the healthy relationships in your life to grow and build trust, you may have to get rid of the unhealthy ones. Change is difficult if you're still around the same people and places you were when you were using. The temptations can be powerful, and the possibility of relapse is always present. With sobriety, you have to alter your environment to be in one that supports your recovery.

Start with realistic expectations about what you're willing to do now.

Forgive yourself as you seek forgiveness from others. Give your loved ones the time they need to go through their healing process, and give yourself the time you need. So often, people want to rush and make things better because dealing with the old or the present is complex, and can be disappointing. But for the healing to be deep and complete, it takes time to go under the surface and make repairs. If it were physical healing, a deep cut that needed stitches, it would take time and a trained medical provider to make sure it closes and heals properly. The top of a wound may look fine because it's closed and stopped bleeding, but underneath, the skin still hasn't finished coming together and sealing tightly. That's why stitches must be removed a week or so later, to ensure that the cut is closed and not infected, that it's healed, or as close to fully recovered as possible.

It takes time before the wound is closed, and the scar forms around the skin. With time, the scar becomes lighter, sometimes blending in with the skin color so that no one wouldn't'tice it if you didn't say anything. That's the beauty of the healing process: you can be healed to the point that people — whether they know you or not —can't tell unless you share that one time you had a wound or injury in that area. Think about someone you know who's shared about their life, and until then, you had no idea they'd once struggled with addiction or had something traumatic happen in their life.

35

When the healing work is done, that person looks, thinks, and acts like a different being. Your life too can be repaired and made new. Give yourself the time and the chance to make it happen.

13

Your do-over is waiting; second chances are a part of your Hero's Journey

Starting over is the right option — giving yourself permission to start anew, and to make up your mind not to stop moving forward. There are days when you won't want to move forward. You'll have times when rehashing in your head everything that went wrong, why it went wrong, and how this could happen is all that you want to do.

Before this starts to spiral downward, you'll need to interrupt and change your thinking to a positive option. Your positive alternative is to focus your thoughts on what your new life will look like once you start over.

Some feelings will creep up that you want to fight away, and the sense of failure is one. Remind your mind and heart that a relationship that fails doesn't mean that *you're* a failure. Feelings aren't always an accurate indicator of what's going on. One temporary feeling isn't the complete picture of how and who you are. Some feelings will come and go; thoughts will come and go. We must choose not to attach ourselves to them. Choose to let that feeling or thought pass through. Sometimes it will take a few attempts, but it will pass.

Get up and start moving in the direction of your dreams, in the direction of your new start.

When you plot your do-over, begin by being honest about what you want this time around. What will you not accept, and what decisions were made that didn't turn out how you expected? Get the correct type of support in your life. Some people will prevent change and fight to maintain things as they're because it's comfortable and safe. Accept that this won't be easy; change is difficult, which is why so many of us avoid change.

There appears to be no risk in things staying the same, which is, however, the biggest lie of all. Every living thing needs to grow; if it doesn't expand or evolve, it will be in distress. Think of old businesses you once knew; imagine the old days, when things like your cell phone didn't exist. Your car would be a big gas-guzzler. You'd have to write notes and mail letters, your shopping for a gift would take hours, and then you'd have to find time to deliver the gift or wrap it yourself to carry to the post office.

Your food would take hours to cook or have to be heated on a stove. On vacation, you'd have to buy a disposable camera and wait a week to develop the photos if they came out on film. Things staying the same isn't desirable; it's just easier and less frightening. You need change, and life requires growth.

To start over, you'll need a plan, like a road map to help you get from where you're now to where you want to go. If you're not sure what to do next, this is an excellent time to dream. Of course, you may think to yourself, "I have to make a decision," but it's not as simple as just saying it.

You have to make the decision and act on the choice you make. You have to work on the decision to keep growing and moving forward when things start going against you. That's what makes it easier to *say* than to *do*.

Put yourself intentionally in new places and spaces that allow you to make new friends. For instance, joining a support group provides a profound way to make friends with people who share the struggle with you. Finding groups that are doing active things you like to do can be a way to make friends and build new relationships around activities.

Use something natural to combat the awkward feelings that come with building new relationships. We all begin scared, but realize that everyone is intimidated by meeting new people and starting new relationships. You'll have doubts along the way, but that's okay and very natural; uncertainty doesn't mean disaster is on the way. It just means there's a risk — so there can be a reward as well.

14

You can rewrite the story of your life, making your next chapter the best

Some of us are born into a nightmare we didn't create, born innocent and just trying to survive the day: Children who are born to drug-addicted parents. Living life as a caretaker for an alcoholic parent, worried about the night coming because they're uncertain if someone is coming to abuse them in the dark. Moving from place to place, living days without food or shelter, and never knowing if mom or dad is in a good or bad mood today.

Hoping to find relief at school and getting there and finding another type of harassment waiting, not being able to find peace either at school or home until we were gone from both. Now, out of the home, the nightmares still creep in; thoughts, memories, and pain. But hope is also there, the hope of turning it around, faith that our story doesn't have to end the way it began. New beginnings and new endings. New ways of framing what happened to us: it wasn't our fault. It was just what happened.

This is the time you say to yourself, "The perpetuating of pain and dysfunction in my family ends with me." The hope comes from believing that it's now your turn to create, plan, and tell your story the way you have imagined it would be. You can rewrite your story and change the story of your entire family. You can make your name respectful, honorable, bringing pride and hope to yourself and your family.

Your new chapter can read, "I made it out and succeeded despite the problems and challenges at home." Now, live and write your adventure story.

We can't pretend the nightmare didn't happen, and that it doesn't come into our minds over and over. The nightmare can cause you to get stuck; it can leave you feeling paralyzed, drained, and discouraged. But the nightmare is limited to the past if you do the work to heal. You can imagine a better future and take action to make that better future a reality. The result of healing, planning, and becoming what you believe takes time, but the outcome is fantastic. You can stop the movie of the past from playing over and over again.

So many people talk about going to find themselves. You're not lost; your true self is buried under the layers of life circumstances. The layers of pain, other people's stuff, has crowded your life and caused the real you to become silent. Your mind and body took all the energy and creativity you had available and used it to survive the situation you were in. It's no wonder you're tired; it's not a mystery why dealing with life caused you to take shortcuts. You had to protect yourself.

When life is happening at a fast and extreme pace all the time, the resources we need are all working to help us survive; and when an opportunity to sit, relax, or zone out comes, we take it. We take the opportunity because we need to recharge and find the energy and spirit to get back into the fight.

Who you are has taken a back seat to who you needed to be in order to survive the situation you were in.

Now the crisis is over, the real you is needed, and it's time to come forth and be who you are. It's time to create yourself with the wisdom, strength, and insight you've gained; it's time to build your new life and your great future.

It's time to be the hero in your story and become the hero for someone else. Make the next chapters of your life the best, because you've already done the hard part: you survived. Don't quit living now, because you have a great movie to star in: welcome to your life redone! Amaze yourself and inspire others; you can rewrite the script of your life to reflect a hero's story and a Hero's Journey. *Your* journey.

15

If you're not here, you'll miss the opportunity to see your children, your partner, and the life you've always wanted

Young parents start with the dream of what their family and best life will be. Imagining being the kind of parent they always wanted to have, having a picture as they get older of an ideal mate. Even if they don't verbalize it, there's a belief that their life will turn out as they'd hoped. They were thinking and imagining the possibilities.

If you're not alive, how will you ever see this dream come true? How will you ever get to meet your ideal partner or find the person who will understand you? If you're not here, how will you get to see the one who accepts and loves you like no one else can? Someone out there can understand how you think when you get quiet, excited, what the twitch in your eye means.

Someone is waiting to meet you who cares and will care enough to read between the lines when you say you're okay or not okay. They're the one who's willing to help encourage and support you. Someone willing to sit with you in the darkness and help you find your way to the light switch and the help you need to make a lasting change. There's someone who can be your friend, and not manipulate or use you.

By not staying in the adventure of life, you miss the chance to see a *great* life.

Right now, you might be in the beginning or middle of your life story, but you're *not* in the end; you haven't seen the good things waiting for you. The right people are coming into your life to help you experience it differently, to see what a good life, free of drama, looks and feels like. Don't miss your turn to have good things happen. There's a friendship waiting for you with someone willing to learn from you. It's possible, if you desire a happy life with someone who loves you — but you have to stay in the game to find them.

The best part of your life is on the other side of this current problem or difficulty. You'll need to believe, to be willing to do the work to help you heal, and to be available to possibilities. Move forward one step at a time, *one inch* if necessary, because even that's progress. Don't believe the lie that you can't have a healthy relationship.

Just because you've never seen a healthy relationship, don't believe the lie that you can't be a good parent or good spouse. If you've never experienced healthy parenting or learned the qualities of a good spouse. that doesn't mean you don't possess the know-how. Becoming good at something is about developing the skill and having a heart that's willing to try. It begins with the desire to be a good parent and a great spouse, and you feed that desire, love, and train with others who are doing it well. You can develop good relationship skills, starting with a willing heart, and continue with small, purposeful steps in the right direction. You can learn to be whoever you need to be for your future family and life.

44

Stay in the game. Don't give up hope for your future. Rise toward your future, full speed ahead, and don't take what's in front of you for granted. It's so easy to look at what you *don't* have rather than appreciate or value what you do have. That way of thinking, that lack of value and appreciation can leave you feeling inadequate. You're *more* than adequate. Don't overlook or discount yourself. Appreciate what you have and where you're in life as you move toward more.

One of the most valuable habits and tools to make life better is the ability to appreciate what you have: gratitude. Sometimes we're slow at appreciating what we've because of impatience. It's hard to be grateful when we want to get to the end, the big stuff. It can be challenging to appreciate simply waking up if you're waiting for the big moment of opening up gifts on Christmas morning. The small miracles or nice things you already have — compared to what you're waiting for — may not be enough to satisfy you, because you're distracted by wanting the next big thing.

Appreciate the small things now, the little things, and don't give up. You'll get to experience both in life: the joy of the little miracles or gifts in life *and* the fun and over-the-top feelings that come with the most significant gifts of a loving family and a positive future. If you give up now, you'll miss seeing the excellent future in store for you. Your dream of belonging to a family, of having an excellent life, hasn't happened yet. It will. Don't quit five minutes before the miracle.

16
Your tribe is waiting for you to show up

You'll miss finding your tribe, people who think like you, their acceptance, understanding, and love. The people who make up your tribe are out there waiting for you to find them, for you to discover the possibility, the connections.

It's a basic human need to have a group of individuals we can feel connected to, people who understand and accept us. If you've tried to get those needs met by people who couldn't do so, the effects can be devastating. Not everyone is capable of accepting you, or equipped to understand you.

You don't need to be accepted or loved by many, only accepted and loved by one or a few. It takes time to find the right people who understand, accept, and bring out the best in you. The people who are happy spending time with you. If you had this once and lost it because of something you or they did, don't lose heart. You can find your tribe, your people, or the one person again. It will take a resource called *time* — and a second one called *hope*.

Being received into someone else's life should be a big deal and take time, because you want it to be right and meaningful. We don't want to go and have our hearts broken or disappointed over and over again; that's why you want to form relationships *slowly* to find out if that person is worth your trust.

Ask yourself: Is this person worthy of hearing my secrets, holding my heart, of seeing me when I'm vulnerable? How has this person treated others? Have they protected other people close to them? Have been they generous, thoughtful, and loving in their relationships?

Other people in this world are like you. Are they kind and forgiving when they're hurt? Are they judgmental, or accepting? You might be thinking, I don't like myself; why would I like them or want to be with them if I don't want to be with myself?

There are other people who are similar to the best parts of you, the side of you that you're proud of, that makes you unique. You can find them; you don't have to be alone or feel like an outcast for the rest of your life. There are people out there who share all kinds of unique interests. For your growth and life success, you want to find people focused on the positive interest that will help you grow, laugh, and enjoy life.

17

When you get stronger, your giants aren't going to look so big

One thing you'll find to be true is that your giants (stress, people, overwhelming circumstances) don't look so big as you get mentally and emotionally stronger. For example, for some people during the holidays, going back to a childhood home they grew up in is a source of anxiety and stress. I remember for many years as a kid going a few blocks away to a grocery store, and from there, I would walk home. It felt like the store was miles away, and when I got back to our house, it looked big and intimidating.

As an adult, I went back there. The house looked small on the inside, and the furniture was old and looked so small. The stairs had looked so long and gigantic when I was a child. Even the bathroom was now miniature. Compared to how I saw things all these years growing up, life has taken on a different perspective now that I'm as big as my giants. When I look at reality now, it doesn't intimidate me as it did before. As you take steps to work on the things that hold you down, the stressors in your life that make it seem overwhelming, you'll start to grow emotionally and mentally stronger.

Working through your painful past in therapy equips you with coping skills and understanding of your behaviors and helps strengthen you. It can help shrink those giants in your life down to size.

Think to yourself, "I'm not four, seven, or ten years old, and I have a say in my life". We've made the old giants (stress, fear, rejection, anxiety) so big, so strong, and we can't think of how we're going to defeat them. When the memories come back, it feels like we're losing the fight. Separate what's authentic from false and take a mental picture of that.

Living in the present and letting go of the past's hold over our lives is easier said than done, but it's not impossible. Finding safe, sound counsel to work through the issues of your past can help you defeat the giant stressors in your life.

The thing that once held you back can become a memory with no power to harm you, no ability to control your day and your thought life, and no power to influence your emotions. It's possible to live free from emotional and spiritual bondage, anxiety, and depression. You can heal, be free and victorious — and the healing can start today. Start now. It begins with the decision to take action to get the help you need now.

18
Your hope can and will grow every day

Hope is grown from a little thought, a little desire that things can and will be better one day. You start to build your hope by saying and realizing that the steps you're taking are moving you toward winning. With just a little effort, you can begin to retrain your way of thinking. You can start by saying, "I'm winning right now with the words that come out of my mouth." "I'm winning right now by reading this book, by listening or watching positive messages." The little energy that you might feel is enough to start to move forward.

The Bible says that just a little mustard seed of faith can move mountains when you're facing mountain size sadness and depression. It takes only a mustard seed of hope to keep going — a tiny seed that can grow into a 20-foot-tall tree in the harsh, dry ground, and grow to provide shelter. This type of seed grows very slowly. Hope starts small, and grows slowly, but it can protect you in difficult times.

The best part of your hope is the willingness to believe change is possible. You gain more confidence as the days go on. You have the secret ingredient. Take it, and get into a new environment and surroundings. Get with others that will help your seeds of hope grow.

Don't try to do it by yourself. For example, in order to farm correctly, we need to ask the farmer, What's the best soil to plant my seed so I can see a harvest?

Where's the best place to put your hope so it might grow, the best atmosphere for you to be in? You can grow stronger, become more courageous, and build a desire to move forward in the right environment. Everybody has a place they need to be so that seeds of hope will grow.

19
Give yourself the permission and the gift of time, and things can and will get better

Time is your friend, but it can feel like an enemy. Sometimes it will make you upset because things are taking too long to change. It will also act like an enemy working against you, not enough time with loved ones or friends, too much time trying to graduate when a two-year degree takes four years. Whether time is working in your favor or against your goals, it demands respect. When you cast it aside by playing video games from sunup to sundown, or being blackout drunk all day or night, time will race by, and you can't get it back. We may fail to recognize time needs respect and to use it wisely.

Time is on your side if you plan. If you live without a plan, without discipline, then your life will be working toward something else — or towaard another person's idea, and not working for *your* goals. Your hopes and dreams matter, and are valuable. Time is a precious resource, the currency needed to make things happen. Right now, you may think, "I'm feeling unhopeful, and the only dreams I have are nightmares." Give yourself the investment of time to get the counseling needed to turn this sense around. You can use the time you have to create a dream, and to build hope.

See time as valuable, and give yourself the time you need to plan, heal, and rebuild your life. With time on your side, making small positive changes will help to turn negative emotions around because you'll be taking control.

Sleeping through your day will add to feelings of sadness, hopelessness, and fatigue. Playing hours of video games will provide you with some moments of laughter or fun, but it will numb you, too — and the minute the game stops, feelings of sadness, guilt, shame, or sleepiness will return. You'll be left feeling unsatisfied, and regretting the time lost. Hours on social media will leave you feeling a range of emotions, primarily negative ones. Watching until you've lost hours isn't satisfying when you have other important things left undone. When you can't remember what you were supposed to get done — when you don't value your time — you're not valuing yourself.

Start by changing how you use your time. Have a plan for your day. To make this plan work, don't allow people to interrupt if they're not helpful, or not on board with the plan. Don't let video games, binge television watching, or social media surfing eat up your time. Plan your day sober from any alcohol, substances, or self-abusing behavior, and you'll begin to feel in control of your day, little by little.

Time to think, plan, and make another decision will help you come out on top. Give yourself time to consider another option, to make a backup plan. Success won't come when you're valuing others above yourself. You're worth the investment; don't give your time away to things or to people that won't help you achieve your goals. Take control by taking back your time and being deliberate about how you spend every hour of your day.

20
You haven't had your "mic drop" moment yet

A "mic drop" moment is when you speak the truth as you experience it and allowe it to be heard by others without fear. This is when you talk and don't hold back the words, or worry about how people will take what you said, or stop short of expressing yourself because of intimidation. A mic drop moment is when you make an important point that helps others reflect critically on what they believe is right. It's when you're unapologetically yourself.

Don't die without living and speaking your truth; you deserve to be heard, acknowledged, and received. Your life story may provoke anger and annoy some people, but that doesn't matter. It deserves to be heard. You have to be alive to bear witness to your story, without judging it as "good" or "bad." You deserve to authentically experience this moment.

What if your speaking up and speaking out leads to the freedom of others? What if being who you are gives others permission others to become who they're supposed to be? Mic drop moments take time to develop. We don't just show up with the wisdom, insight, and courage needed to have this moment. We grow it over time, take time to develop, and permit ourselves to be who we're,. If you think about the best meal you've ever had, chances are this meal was prepared by an expert who practiced making that meal repeatedly. They took their time to prepare the meal, possibly a day before cooking or baking it. A delicious, good meal takes time to prep, and time to cook.

Being at your best will take time. Give yourself the gift of patience. Take the time you need to invest in yourself, and give yourself the right to grow into the skills or the new way of thinking you're trying to develop. Don't fall into the trap of making a decision and assuming you'll achieve this significant goal or change in your life tomorrow. Any big dream, any new way of operating will take time.

The new you'll not be made tomorrow; you'll shed some things, add others and slowly become the new you, the *you* that you've always been inside, deep down. When others who have started on the same journey quit working toward their goals, you must keep going. Perseverance takes recognizing and acknowledging that change and growth will take time. Give yourself the grace and time you need. You won't become an expert at thinking positively overnight; you'll have to work on it every day to think positively, train yourself to feel differently, and make other choices.

21
Have you tried acceptance?

We fight change, avoid difficulties and put up defenses against anything that might be a threat. But have you tried acceptance? This is a complex concept to receive; many people think acceptance means condoning what's taken place. On the other hand, we also tend to equate acceptance with weakness. Acceptance doesn't mean either one of these. True acceptance is a path to freedom, freeing your mind, heart, and emotions from being tied to issues. If you haven't learned to accept, you're powerless to make a difference.

The idea of acceptance is an essential part of the recovery experienced by many in Alcoholics Anonymous (AA) and other Twelve Step programs. It's a powerful concept indeed because of the freedom and peace you gain from integrating acceptance into your life. Acceptance doesn't mean saying what you choose to accept is either good or bad; it's simply understanding and allowing the facts to be what they're. Acceptance doesn't mean that the facts may not change over time due to other factors. Accepting the reality of where you're can help fight the frustration you feel if something hasn't changed.

When you're at peace with recognizing your limitations, letting go of all expectations will feel like an emotional weight being lifted. Expectations are at the core of your pain. The dictionary defines expectations as "a strong belief that something will happen or be the case in the future."

Expectations that are unmet and unfilled are dangerous because of the amount of hope or belief we placed in them.

We get into relationships with certain expectations: "This person is going to make me feel good, make me forget my problems, love me the way I need to be loved." "This person is going to make me happy all the time; I'll be so happy that I won't be depressed anymore." "This person will always know what I want." These may sound like expectations you've had. If your relationship has changed, then you understand the downside of unmet expectations.

Expectations aren't unhealthful; they begin as a desire inside us, trying to get filled. An expectation grows as a hope that someone or something is going to fill that space or meet that need we've inside us. Then it becomes a "must": they must serve this need, which leads to disappointment and frustration when the need is still there, and the other person can't or won't meet the demand.

When the expectation is coming from us, we become frustrated with ourselves because we can't accomplish what we're trying to get done. Or, we become upset with ourselves because it takes years to change a habit. After all, we're not making the improvements quickly enough. This is the moment to begin by first accepting yourself: accepting that you're not perfect, that you can't do everything, that you're human, and that you therefore make mistakes. You'll make mistakes often, and afterward the errors will seem obvious and easy to avoid; but nevertheless, you'll stumble. The answer to the problem will seem simple, but that doesn't mean it will be easy.

If I tell you to sit in a chair and not move for one hour, that seems straightforward. It's simple: relax, and don't move for one hour. Now, is it easy? No. It's not easy because we get distracted, and it's not easy because our phone will ring, or a text will come through. We may get tired or hungry, or have to use the bathroom; we're not always sure of the instructions, our minds wander, and our moods and emotions go up and down. There are many reasons why sitting in a chair may be simple — but it's not easy. The same thing is true for acceptance. It seems simple enough: if I accept myself just as I'm, then I can take others the way they're. Not easy, but a simple concept. Practice letting go of expectations, and accepting yourself and others exactly as you are at this moment.

22
You're a solution, not a problem

"My family thinks I'm the problem, the outcast, the black sheep." Maybe you challenge the family system, their way of operating, and their beliefs. Taking away the judgment on your behavior and looking at the possibilities, perhaps some of the challenges you bring are forcing everyone in the family to check their premises and consider making changes. Some of the changes may be positive, and some may not. Your thinking, acting, and way of being are not "right" or "wrong," but they may challenge the family's way of thinking and interacting. This challenge can help positive change to take place.

If you deal with labels other people have placed on you, now is the time to peel them off. Some of the names used against loved ones are: loser, problem child, unwanted, incompetent, junkie, criminal, failure, hopeless, idiot, not-good-enough, lost, broken, slow, freak, rebel, arrogant, dumb, hoe, liar, embarrassment, reject, thief, stubborn, lazy, procrastinator, needy, difficult, desperate, scared.

These labels are only words used to describe a behavior based on someone else's opinion or perspective. These labels aren't the truth about who you are, and they don't serve to tell the whole story. Some are lies made to tear down your self-esteem; some describe how you once behaved, or something you did — but not who you are consistently or at the core of your being.

63

There's a significant difference between who you are and what you do. You can do something or act in a certain way that doesn't align with what you believe, who you are, or what you value. You can be a person that loves children, but when you're tired and frustrated, you may yell at them because you don't know what else to do to get time alone or make the environment quiet. You can be someone who cares about other cultural or ethnic groups, yet in a heated argument say something derogatory about another person.

The labels and words that others carelessly and hurtfully throw around are just that, and no more. You can choose not to accept the words. You can refuse to make them a part of your biography. Other people's opinions, interpretations, fears, or insecurities aren't your problem, and *not* part of your story. Choose to let the words roll off your back. Choose to allow the words not to enter your ears or stick to your mind. What others think is a thought, not a fact, and not your reality.

Don't trap your mind or emotions in the jail that's built by their words. You don't have the time or energy to bury yourself under the heavy burden of words which others target you. Don't take on their labels, and don't let them define who you are. If your behavior is now forming a pattern that would make someone believe this is who you are, acknowledge if you've done something that needs to change. Recognize your part and make a change, but don't accept and live out that name or label yourself, because the label doesn't belong.

Labels aren't the truth of who you are inside or what you value.

If you're having difficulty letting go of names others choose to use on you, here is one way to think differently about the labels below. These aren't excuses for any behavior, but a different way of looking at these hurtful names.

Label	Different perspective
Loser	I haven't found the thing I'm good at yet.
Problem child	I knows that something isn't right, but I won't live a lie. I'm trying to understand how to make it in a world that doesn't make sense yet.
Unwanted	I'm a diamond wrapped in coal, the surprise you didn't know you needed.
Incompetent	I'm in the wrong job or given the wrong task for my skills. When the right job finds my skills — Watch out, world!
Junkie	I'm trying to forget, escape, or soothe the pain with the wrong medicine. I'm one decision away from positive change.
Criminal	I'm a creative, impulsive individual, working on decision-making skills. I still have a hard time waiting for reward. or not responding when provoked.
Failure	I'm just one try away from success, but I need others to come along see how it's possible, and for them to stay encouraged.
Hopeless	I can find hope in any situation if I look with

	eyes of grace. No one that's living and breathing is beyond hope.
Idiot	I'm the right person but perhaps the wrong fit. I'm capable and need a different way of learning and understanding. I'm valuable and necessary in the right situation. Those who can see me nurture and respect the gift that I offer, and the treasure that I'm.
Lost	I'll find my place where I belong at the right time. I'm exploring and I'll find my way.
Broken	Something new and valuable is being created from my pain and struggle. I'll bend, but I won't break. I'm always getting better.
Slow	I take the time needed to get things right the first time. "Faster" doesn't mean better or smarter.
Freak	I'm spectacular! I may not be for everyone — who is— but I'm amazing to anyone who can truly see me.
Rebel	I just another way of doing things, and my own way of seeing life.
Arrogant	I need to protect what's important to me and unseen by you.

Label	Different perspective
Dumb	Everyone is right sometimes, and wrong other times. No one knows everything, and no one knows what I experience and believe.
Hoe	I have a story you don't know, and may not understand; I'm not limited by your morals.
Liar	I need to hide and protect something vulnerable. Deceit has kept me safe in the past.
Reject	My purpose is different than yours, and waiting to be discovered. I'm a treasure who's still unseen and underappreciated.
Thief	I have a need, and I'm afraid to ask because it makes me feel vulnerable — and it may come at a price I'm not sure I can or want to pay.
Stubborn	I'm just not sure if this is safe or good for me — so please wait. I have some reservations about this: What if I lose something? What if I change my mind? What if I fail?
Lazy	I'm uncertain, and I need to be convinced this will work or be right for me. I haven't found something that moves me.
Procrastinator	I'm scared, and the fear paralyzes and exhausts me.
Needy	Love and certainty is what I want and must

have.

Difficult	This isn't for me; it doesn't match my values and priorities. I choose not to try and make it fit.
Desperate	Help me, without judging or condemning me, Be a friend.
Scared	I tried and failed before. I lost something, and I'm just trying to avoid feeling that pain.

I want to leave you with a quote from Eleanor Roosevelt, who said, "No one can make you feel inferior without your consent." Labels and harsh words can cause feelings of inferiority — and turn your emotions upside down. Don't give into someone else's opinion. Acknowledge when your behaviors go against your values or aren't suitable for your life. Then, work on not repeating these behaviors by practicing new actions which reflect your values. Remember that actions can change, and your response is more about how you think, interpret, and respond to what's happening around you. Your reaction isn't who you are; it's often a quick emotional response to a perceived offense or threat, or to a need.

Change your perspective. Sometimes, family members of other people close to you have labeled you as the problem. But consider this: what if *you're* the cure, the solution, the help your family needs? What if something was missing or needed, and you were born as a solution? What if, while treating your medical condition, a cure was found for someone else? What if getting the help you need leads your family to seek help, and healing comes to your family?

You're not the label anyone else tries to place on you. Don't accept other people's labels — and if one of these labels sticks to you, peel it off and reveal the precious being you are.

23
We're better off with you, not without you

When you make the statement, "They're better off without me," you're making assumptions because you don't know all the ways you impact the lives of other people. The thought of someone being better off without you is rooted in low self-worth, and in the mistaken assumption that your input or presence has worsened a given situation. It's also a reaction to disappointment. When we try to make something happen by will power, or wanting it to happen, we open ourselves up and become vulnerable to distress. We create an expectation.

We can be disappointed by trusting in outcomes that don't come to be. Disappointment comes after making plans, because we turn possibilities and situations into future realities without anticipating, "What if this doesn't happen?" It's always great to plan, and to get excited about what we hope will become reality. This expectation of positive results helps us move forward and take healthy risks.

Nonetheless, it's essential to prepare emotionally and mentally for risk by sprinkling our hope with realistic expectations. "I'm hopeful that I'll get this job, yet I know that many others are applying, and the competition will be fierce. Therefore, I'm preparing for the next opportunity in the event that I don't get this one." "I'm hopeful and expect my marriage will work out and be great. I'm also realistic, and

I know that my life isn't over if it doesn't work out. If it doesn't work out I can bounce back."

We deal with disappointment by not allowing our feelings about not getting what we want or expect to consume our thoughts and control our emotions. We deal with the frustration by acknowledging whether we could have done better, and by applying what we've learned next time. When we're young, our disappointment focuses on what others did or didn't do that caused the issue; but as we mature, a decision must be made to grow—the decision to own our mistakes, miscommunication, or misinterpretation. Take responsibility if you failed to prepare, or if you took the opportunity for granted. Take accountability for your missteps, misinformation, or your lack of realistic expectations.

Disappointment comes in many forms: we're disappointed because we did something that didn't match our values; we felt let down by a close friend who didn't keep their promise; a relationship didn't go as planned; a coworker stood by while we got yelled at for something that they failed to do; we failed to follow through on a commitment we made to ourself. These are all examples of occasions where discouragement can quickly settle in and make us feel inadequate, unreliable, and unworthy. We make up a story in our mind about the situation without any facts to back it up. To turn this around and stop the mental spiral into discouragement, be truthful. Don't be deceived by negative thoughts. And when you lose, don't lose the lesson.

73

Learn from past mistakes and be balanced in your future expectations around people and opportunities. You're worthy, you're needed — and yes, this world is better off with you in it than it would be without you.

24

You're stronger than you feel and smarter than you think, and you have what it takes to make it

Don't allow people who aren't supportive of you to have access to your heart or manipulate your feelings of self-worth. We all want to be and feel hopeful. Don't attempt to convince people; show them compassion and understanding while you move forward. They don't have to give you permission to move on and achieve your dreams. You have to permit yourself to grow, and then take action to make it happen. You'll not experience or know what you can handle until you take the chance and try.

The first attempt is only one in many. It doesn't matter if you try and don't get very far; you have to keep at it. You'll knock down the wall in front of you brick by brick, and sometimes you have to chip away at the wall inch by inch, layer after layer. Your persistence is why and how you'll win, the tenacity to say, "No matter what, I'll keep moving forward, I'll win." This is the type of mindset that gives you the fuel to win and grow stronger.

Growing smarter comes with applying the wisdom you gain and learning more as you examine your mistakes. Mistakes are meant to be reviewed to learn from them so you can change your direction and build. Find the people who think like you. Build a base, a group that understands and connects with you.

When you want to change or grow, find people who think differently when it's time to produce results. Surround yourself with people who act differently. Life doesn't guarantee roses, but they do come and they come with thorns. Life is full of challenges and changes, and you were born with what you need to handle them.

25

You can make a positive decision for your future: stop letting others control your emotions

Emotions don't tell the whole story about the situation facing you at this moment. Feelings can be controlled; they can change in a moment and pass once we acknowledge, choose to accept and release them. Don't neglect yourself emotionally and physically; don't put someone else in charge of you. That won't work. If you're waiting for someone who's arrogant, distant, or in denial to respond or change, you're placing them in control of your emotions.

When someone is abusive mentally, they're not in a place to offer you what you need. If they're hurting you, they can't love you or be there for you. Don't place your life on hold, waiting and hoping they will change. Some people in your life are only capable of giving you the bare minimum — or worse. They may be operating from a place of pain, loss, or trauma, and not have the capacity to provide you with what you need.

When someone has endured a life of abuse or dysfunction, they're not capable of giving you the love and care you need until they learn how to safely meet their own needs. They can only give and teach you what they know. Don't spend your life, energy, time, and money trying to get something from them that they can't give to you.

This energy spent will leave you tired, angry, empty, and in more mental and emotional pain. It's like someone giving you an empty bottle of water and telling you, "Drink."

They don't have the drink of water to give, and they don't realize the bottle of water they're offering is empty. When they give you the bottle, they think, "It's full; you should be happy I gave it to you." Some people will even say, "If you can't get water out of that bottle, it's your fault." This is what we call crazymaking: a person who's setting you up to lose. Don't take the bait.

Give yourself permission to move past this relationship and find a healthy one that can meet your needs. Give yourself permission to invest the time and energy into yourself, and love yourself so that love received from others is extra. Learn to accept what's good or positive and let go of the rest.

Acknowledge the feelings of loss around that relationship, the loss of a desire to get more from that person. You're valuable, even if they weren't able to see or acknowledge it. Removing that person from your life is setting a reasonable boundary. Not everyone is worthy of holding your heart, or having a place in your life.

Limiting your exposure or removing yourself from toxic people is healthy. Don't let them continue to have a place in your life and damage what's already fragile and in need of healing. Maybe their role or purpose in your life is complete, and now it's time to make new relationships. Build the family you want and create the relationships you need. Get a healthy start by making and developing new and positive relationships. You can withstand the old feelings and make a new, positive decision for your future.

26
To Experience Yourself Healthy, Active, and Thriving

Start moving your body, and your mind will follow. How are you feeling physically? Is your physical state relaxed, tense, or tired? How we feel has a direct impact on how we think. We can change how we feel in a moment by catching the feeling, and mentally and physically making the shift. Mel Robbins describes a great example of how to do this in her book, *The 5 Second Rule: Transform your Life, Work, and Confidence with Everyday Courage.* The 5-second rule involves changing your emotional state by taking a physical action after five seconds. You can find out more by reading the book or looking her up on YouTube. Changing your physical condition — for example, off the couch, or out of bed — will change your mental and emotional state because your body has to concentrate on doing something different. Your body is moving in another direction or taking on a simple task, and sends the message, "We're moving forward; we're busy, we're productive." This is a positive step in the right direction.

There are other ways, as well, to change your physical state. You can get up and start saying positive things to yourself: "I'm smart." "I can handle anything that comes my way." "I'm getting better." "I'm feeling better." "I'll conquer this thing: I won't let depression take over; I won't allow sadness to control my life; I choose to live and not die; I want to become someone great. I decide to change!"

You want to change your physical state from angry or agitated to calm and peaceful, from down and slumped shoulders to excited and head up. You want to look at your movements and posture, and change them to reflect how you want to feel — not how you're feeling right now.

27
To know how it feels to live emotionally sober and drama-free

Our feelings can lie to us. Sometimes, we feel angry, sad, or agitated, and we may not know why. Sometimes, the feelings come, and we move through them without getting stuck. You can control your emotions by the meaning or reason you give to something that has happened. Say that someone cuts you off in traffic, or doesn't hold the door open for you, letting it slam shut on you. Feelings of anger are going to form, but if you take a moment and tell yourself, "That person must have an emergency, that's why they let the door slam and didn't look back," then you've changed the meaning or reason for this incident. If you think, "This person must be having a bad day, that's why they cut me off … I understand because I've had bad days or have been in a rush before," this new thought changes the meaning of what happened — and your emotions will slow down and change with the new thought or purpose you've given to this incident.

Start by purposely thinking about something else, something that makes you feel the opposite of how you may feel right now. For instance, look up pictures on your phone that make you smile. Find a quote that gives you feelings of hope.

Here are some steps to getting and feeling better, and to changing your emotional state:

Identify "stinking thinking" by remembering times you've engaged in the behavior. "Stinking" thoughts — unproductive, negative ideas —take away from your energy. However, they're not necessarily harmful, unless they keep coming into your mind and you begin to let them control what you'll or won't do. When these thoughts get louder and begin to intrude, that's when they become harmful.

Unproductive thoughts take away your ability to get things done. They stop you in your tracks, and it takes a lot of energy to move past those thoughts and get through your day. You can function, but with limited mental focus, power, or joy.

Destructive thoughts are the most harmful ones. They sound like this: "My life doesn't matter." "Who would miss me, anyway?" "I just cause more problems." "Everyone would be better off without me." "I'd be better off dead." These are dangerous, destructive thoughts that signal you need to get help. These thoughts shouldn't be entertained or allowed to grow in your mind. Get help from a licensed professional in your area, or go to the nearest ER (emergency room). Seek help in dealing with these thoughts, especially if they come often or on a regular basis, or if you've attempted suicide in the past.

If you think you may be suffering from depression, *please* seek professional help as soon as possible. Don't just say, "This will pass." See someone who can help you figure out the level of support you might need, and who can help you determine if this is a temporary crisis or a long-term issue.

28

You're a friend to someone who might not have one if it weren't for you

We can't underestimate the value of a friend when we're down or feeling alone. You may have friends with whom you haven't shared the thoughts you're having. A friendship isn't tested when everything is good. It's not when you're partying, having fun on vacation, or looking your best that you see what others are made of. You'll get to know the moral character of your friends when you're feeling down, alone, and when you're not friendly or pleasant to be around, but they reach out and try to help anyway.

Ask yourself why you can be a good friend to someone else, but you don't allow them to be a good friend to you. If you ask people, many will say, "one of my best qualities is being a good friend, trustworthy and reliable." The problem is that they're out of balance when they turn around and say, "I don't have anyone I can trust or talk to." They're giving more than they're receiving.

In their relationships, when they're feeling down, depressed, or hopeless, they don't have someone they can talk to and confide in. That's like having a pitcher filled with water that pours out into other cups and never gets refilled. It will run dry, and eventually have nothing more to offer — even though it needs just as much as those around it.

85

You're a friend to someone who might not have a friend if you weren't there for them. Allow someone to show you they can be the friend you need, and let them know honestly about the struggle you're having, about the feelings and the thoughts that have come into your mind. The strength of relationships is tested with life circumstances, and many get stronger and better in hard times, while others fade away or break apart. It's okay to see if your friendship is worth the investment of time, emotions, and experiences by being free and sharing the truth. A good friend will be there to listen and help, even if that help means getting professional care that could save your life. Let your friend become a reliable friend by allowing them to help you. Real friends want the best for each other, no matter what.

It will help if you stay in the fight, because someone else is counting on you to be a friend to them and not give up. Your friendship could help bring hope to them and to yourself — if you allow yourself to believe it.

29
You haven't tried every food, or experienced every country — there's so much more to explore

Let this be your "year of yes." In her book, *Year of Yes: How to Dance It Out, Stand in the Sun and Be Your Own Person,* Shonda Rhimes talks about the many opportunities that were made available to her when she started saying "yes." Are there people in your life who've invited you to dinner, a movie, or a party, and you keep saying "no" to them? Try making this your year of "yes." Try opening yourself up to the possibility of experiencing the joy and connection you want. To feel connected, we've to reach out and give others something to hold on to. Let your hand reach out and grab hold of someone else's by saying yes to the next invitation you get.

You may wonder if someone will remember you, or if others notice you. They do see you; they have recognized you, but have you been rejecting them, or choosing to isolate yourself? When others reach out, do you shrink back and run in the opposite direction? When I've taken the chance to say yes to an event or opportunity in my life, the outcome has been positive. By saying yes, I had an excellent, exciting experience. These small opportunities led to other bigger doors opening.

The life you want can be one right decision away. It can happen, but first you'll have to leave some things behind —

like the limitations of other's people's rules. Determine that you deserve to live the life you want. You can create a *new* life experience, rather than leave the only one you think you have.

You can begin to look forward to trying and doing new things. Learn about what it takes to travel on a budget, and explore developing the skill of playing an instrument or starting a business. You get to choose what desire, passion, or ability you want to go after. You get to go out into the world and experience new people, fun things, ways to live, explore, and go through life.

Life has so much more to offer outside of your job, your neighborhood, and your family. There are people you haven't met who are fascinating — and who are interested in you, and how you think and see the world. There are foods you can't pronounce and haven't tried that would knock your socks off. You might even learn how to cook some of those dishes. There are hunting, fishing, scuba diving, or sailing experiences you haven't tried, and you'll want to go again when you do.

Have you ever:
Seen a glacier
Run with the bulls
Skydived
Flown a plane
Starred in a movie
Salsa danced
Ridden a bull
Coached a team
Tried yoga
Cooked dinner for your close friends
Bungee jumped

Explored other faiths by attending a service

Taken a chance at a poetry slam or amateur comic night

Slept on a beach overnight

Traveled to feed hungry people here or overseas

Taken music lessons

Fostered a shelter pet

Taken photography lessons

Volunteered at a local shelter or nursing home

Gone horseback riding

Joined an amateur acting group

Built and flown a drone with others

Built a house

…?

This is just a small list to start brainstorming all the things in life you could try. There's so much more to the personality that you haven't explored, due to the stress in your life. Why should other people get to have the experiences listed above and not you? It's not a matter of money or time. You can get there. It will take creativity and planning, but any things listed above are within your reach.

It can be done — and trying one thing may lead to accomplishing more. For example, volunteering to help care for poor people can lead to meeting people who may open doors for you in the future and help you accomplish your other dreams. Your trip can guide you to find a meaningful solution to a big problem.

If volunteering isn't for you, then look at fostering a pet. A pet can bring joy to your life with its unconditional love; your pet can give you one reason to get out of bed until you discover other reasons. A pet can open your life up to new friends or a possible soul mate just by going out for a walk every morning.

These experiences can help create hope and momentum in your life. Often we do more for others than we do for ourselves. Invite others into your life by opening yourself up to new experiences. To break out of the rut you're in, you'll have to try something new. It might be intimidating, but it can feed your mind, spirit, and soul as a result. It's time to move forward and change the things you can in order to invite fun and possibilities into your life.

It starts with believing it's possible — and then saying *yes* and going forward to make it happen. There's power in you, opening your mind to the possibilities of trying new things, the opportunity to live life fully awake, open to the good, letting all of the stuff you can't change take a back seat. Become relentless about moving forward and going after your dreams.

30

To learn how to be good to yourself

No one can love you fully if you don't love yourself. You have to be open to receive what others are offering. If you don't believe you deserve the love, you'll act accordingly — by rejecting people trying to love you, by remaining closed off, by hurting others with your words or actions before they can hurt you. It's time to be good to yourself.

Being good to yourself involves taking care of the body that houses your mind and spirit first. If you're not taking care of your body, it will get sick, be tired, shut down, and stop serving you the energy you need to make it through the day.

Treat your body like an expensive car: don't settle for anything harmful being put inside it, and don't allow others to mark it up, beat on it, or take it for a ride whenever they want to. Your body deserves the best care and attention. Your body is a source of pleasure, but not for everyone. Pleasure that's out of control, out of context, or outside of a healthy relationship can break down (rather than build) your physical body. Be intentional about how you let others have access to your body.

You may think that eating an entire tub of ice cream and a large pizza is being good to yourself because it feels good — temporarily. Your body enjoyed the first spoonful or the first two slices, and after that went into overload. All your energy went into breaking down your food, and nothing was left for you to feel motivated.

You feel bloated and tired physically because of the work your body is doing in processing the load you've given it.

Give yourself rest. Sleep is necessary, but too much sleep can be harmful, causing low energy and problems remembering. Oversleeping can be a sign of avoidance, shutting down, or depression. Be good to yourself by sleeping only for as long as you need, and get out of bed. Your body is craving movement, sun, and something new. It's time to bathe, put on clean clothes and get out of the house — even if you're only walking to the library, coffee shop, or park. Getting up and getting moving is one way to be good to yourself. You're giving your mind new thoughts, your body sunlight, and your senses something new to take in. If you've been in a dark, dusty room, your lungs will be thanking you for fresh air. Your joints are happy because of the movement. How about writing down — every day — one good thing you've done to be kind to yourself?

31
To experience exhaling the anger and inhaling love

Anger is the result of a perception that comes after an action or statement, followed by a feeling. This feeling is supported by a belief leading to conclusions and more intense emotions. Anger is seen most often in traffic altercations. For example, someone driving with kids in the car and sideswiped in traffic may perceive the other driver as trying to hurt their family. Feeling disrespected and angry, they chase the perceived offender down and "flip them the bird."

At some point in life, we can become very good at being angry. It's an emotion we know well: like a fast car accelerating from zero to hundred, it comes, easy, smoothly, and so quick that we forget to think. When you use words like a weapon to cut someone who's "in your way," your thinking is blocked by your rage and your actions become robotic. Your mouth opens, your fists clench, and someone is going to feel the brunt of your anger. You may have grown up fighting, or tongue lashing at everyone who you believe gets in your way. Perhaps you were taught that "the best defense is a good offense," with a motto of "hit first, hit hard," and now you're alone as a result.

If people are on edge when you walk in the room ... if, when people speak, they hesitate, not wanting to upset you ... if someone asks you to you remember a time when you weren't angry, and you have to stop and think for a long time ... then anger may be an issue that needs your attention.

Anger is dangerous because it can be very destructive. Anger can cause emotional and physical pain to you and your loved ones. Anger can cause quick decisions with catastrophic, life-changing consequences.

Anger left untreated can turn into depression. Feeling annoyed, hateful, hostile, or vengeful will leave you exhausted. Those feelings can lead to substance abuse and other addictions in your misguided attempt to numb the feelings. Anger, like fire, sucks all the oxygen out of a room, and fuels itself and grows unless it's dealt with. If you feel like anger weighs heavily on your chest, then releasing it is symbolic of exhaling, taking the heaviness away — at potentially great cost. Instead of using the oxygen to increase the anger, use it to inhale more love for yourself and the love others are trying to give you.

When we're angry, it's easy to miss the signs or opportunities other people are giving us: the sign of forgiveness, the opportunity to receive or offer an apology. It's easy to miss the way out of a situation if you're furious. Anger as a trigger is like someone throwing a football to you, and you receive it. You may not want the ball, it could belong to someone else, but when you receive it, you own the opportunity to become angry. Then, you get angry and decide to unleash the fury (rage) or bury the fury inside (depression). When someone is having a hard time managing their anger, they're not looking at option number three: to release the anger.

Letting go of responding in anger isn't saying that the action causing you pain was okay or acceptable. Releasing the anger is about you — not about the other person, and not about what happened. Choosing to release anger is about taking responsibility. Releasing the anger is a choice to be free of engaging in an emotion that will leave you tired, disgusted, pissed off — and stuck. We only have 24 hours in a day, and if you allow some act of disrespect, some gesture or something said to you in seconds to upset you for hours or days, you're cutting yourself a raw deal. You may even wonder, "Can I be angry in my sleep?" Yes, you can be upset in your sleep, and have a restless night because of it. Allowing that act, gesture, or something said to rob you of many hours of peace, rest, or happy memories with your loved ones is self-destructive.

Anger is a choice; your reaction to feeling disrespected, to the pain caused or the perception of loss is a choice. Opportunities will come frequently to get angry and stay angry. But if you're going to enjoy life, you have to exhale, release the anger, and inhale the joy, peace, and forgiveness. You have to decide that life can and should be lived happily. Choose not to be angry with yourself, not to drink or smoke or act away the feelings of anger, but to release them by managing the motions while you're wide awake. When you can manage the feelings without a drug-induced or behavior-induced state, you'll experience being in full control of your moods. The drink, substance, or behavior is only a temporary relief, followed by long-lasting consequences and feelings of shame. The mastering of your emotions is long-term victory; it's the ultimate win, because others don't control your reaction. You control and determine how to respond. When you control the emotion of anger, life stressors aren't as heavy or exhausting. The blanket of control, exhaustion, tension, and suspicion is lifted off your shoulders.

People dealing with anger are quick to be suspicious of the actions of others, waiting to be proven right when someone "causes them" to be upset by triggering something in them. Don't let anyone be the match to light your fire. That fire in you is a passion for expressing yourself. Love for yourself and others should be at the top of your list of things that motivate you. Motivation led by anger doesn't last. In the long run. motivation driven by love can outlast and outperform anything it's put up against. Life is waiting to be experienced with your arms open to receive — instead of your fists clenched, guarding you from everything.

32
To fall in love and stay there

If you're on marriage number three after being cheated on, abandoned, or lied to, love can be a four-letter word. When the track record you have is failure in relationships or marriages, it's easy to fall into the negative spiral of self-pity and bitterness after a breakup: thinking of all the reasons why this happened to you, of all the ways you could have changed or prevented what took place.

If you keep looking back, you'll miss what's ahead of you. Stop replaying the movie in your mind with multiple fantasy endings, and accept the conclusion of what happened. It's okay to feel sad, angry, and empty; these feelings are normal and should be temporary. When they cross over to lasting every day, all day, for long periods of time, that's a sign it's time to get outside help and not try and manage the feelings alone.

Feeling the pain of losing the relationship but staying in that same state of mind is dangerous, and will destroy the possibility of a better future that you could begin now. You have the right to experience love again, and a better type of love from your previous relationship's. You owe it to yourself to try again and start fresh. The person who deserves you, who will understand you, is out there and waiting to meet you.

Getting out of the places that keep you isolated is part of taking the small action steps to make falling in love again possible.

Letting go of the reminders from past relationships is another step, a mental and physical action taken before starting a new relationship. This may involve getting rid of the pictures on your cell phone, deleting phone numbers, removing someone's stuff from your home or apartment. It may mean removing them from your social media accounts and resisting every temptation to call, stalk them, or ask your friends about them. New doors can't open until old ones are closed.

Spend time with new people and get into new activities to allow yourself to make new memories. You have to be in action for change to take place. When you're moving and living life, opportunities will come to you. The best part about letting go and moving on is in learning about yourself. That last relationship may have brought out a side of you that you didn't expect; it may have taken you to a dark and harmful place. A new relationship can help you discover the better, happier side of you if you allow that to happen naturally. Don't look for a clone of your ex or try to mend your broken heart by quickly getting into a new relationship. Resist running from one relationship into another. Take your time, but do it expecting something good to happen.

Give yourself a second chance at experiencing love. What if this next relationship is one that brings out the best in you, and vice versa? What if it turns out you're happier than ever? There are no promises that relationships won't have twists and turns, and some internal emotional work required from you beforehand. Recognize that you can build hope, that you can find the right person for you — a real person, not someone perfect, or without flaws. After all, are you?

This is about developing the positive and confident belief that you'll meet someone who complements your life in a real, healthful way.

<u>Just a couple of tips to help you make a solid leap forward:</u>

Time and distance are required. Avoid calling, visiting, or trying "one more time" to revive a relationship that was toxic. Each time leaving will get harder, and the pain can grow and go deeper.

Remember the good things, but be honest about the bad ones. If the person had an addiction, or was abusive physically or emotionally, no amount of love alone is going to change them. They have to desire and acknowledge they're ready to change. If you're the person who was abusive, let the other person have their freedom to start a new relationship and to heal. Release them emotionally; show compassion, empathy, and true love by allowing them to go and become healed while you pursue your own healing.

33
To experience your gifts and talents

Do you know how much you're capable of accomplishing? If you haven't tried anything new, how do you know if you'd be good at it or not? You haven't begun to explore your potential or experiment with the possibilities of who you can become. There's so much more to you than you give yourself credit for. What have you thought about trying that you haven't yet jumped into? What dream is waiting?

Stop letting doubt, fear or insecurities get in the way. Take the leap and start to do what's necessary to make things happen. Don't just plan and think about it: plan and do. Choose your next step and take things to the next level. If you're in motion, there won't be time for doubt and second-guessing. If you make a mistake, then recognize it, accept and adjust, but never stop moving. It's okay to make mistakes! That's how we learn. *When you lose, don't lose the lesson.*

Every day builds on the last one. If you take one small action step today, and one step every day, by the end of the week you'll have completed seven small tasks and made a big difference in learning and moving forward toward your goals.

Commit to yourself, not with a promise but with a contract. You'll take the next one to five steps by a specific time, and if you don't accomplish a step, have a consequence in place. Take something you enjoy, and don't allow yourself to do it until you achieve the next step of your commitment.

Starting on the road to accomplishing your dreams doesn't have to be a series of great big steps taken all at once. You can start by devoting 15 minutes a day — tops — to learning a new skill. For example, you can start by telling yourself, "For 15 minutes I'm going to practice playing an instrument, then increase slowly the next time. For 15 minutes a day I'll practice, and for another 15 minutes I'll watch a video on how to play. Then I'll take a 45-minute lessons from a professional, and soon I'll have invested 90 minutes daily over five days. That's 450 minutes — or 7 ½ hours — learning a new skill." Do you have 15 minutes to give? Yes, you do — and you can start now. If you're thinking, "I don't own or have what I need," plan to get it. Trade something of value with someone else. Borrow the instrument, or buy it used. Let others know what you're trying to do, and someone will guide you on how to buy, borrow, or trade — so you can get what you need to realize your dreams.

There are other dreams that you can start working on — and it's free. If you have an interest or talent in drawing, painting, writing, or photography, start today with what you have on hand and build from that starting point.

As Henry David Thoreau wrote: "Go confidently in the direction of your dreams! Live the life you've imagined."

34
To learn how to create and hold on to happiness

Do you believe that happiness is possible? That it's something you can reach, feel, and hold on to? Do you think happiness is only for "those people" or "other people," people who are "born happy and optimistic"? Perhaps you're thinking, "Is happiness possible in my situation? Is it possible after failure, after losing everything? Is happiness realistic after pain, rejection, or losing someone? Why do I need to be happy — isn't that for everyone else? I don't feel satisfied, and I don't know how to get happy."

Happiness is possible to get, hold on to, and grow. Happiness isn't about how you feel; it's about how you *think* and how you experience what's around you. If happiness were only a feeling, then most of the world would be chasing it all day, every day.

Happiness is a way of thinking and a state of being, and it's hard to reach when your thoughts are focused on the negative. For instance, if you're worried about money, thinking about how much you should have, used to have, and how much you're paying out every month, it can be overwhelming. A mind consumed by negative thoughts doesn't have room to let positive thoughts grow. When your thoughts are focused on what you don't have or what you've lost, it will be difficult to feel and stay happy. Getting to happiness takes work — but the work is in mind, and the action is practiced every day.

It may feel like ping-pong in your mind as you go back and forth to combat and dispel the negative thoughts with the positive ones.

How do you create happiness? You start with looking for the good things in your life. What's something in your life that you appreciate having? What do you have that others don't? Think of someone that has less than you do. Look around your home: is there something you have which, if you gave it away to someone in need, could help make their life better? Do you remember a time where you had less than what you have now? Finding and staying happy is a practice daily, hourly — a practice of appreciation, changing your perspective, and being mindful of the moment and of positive realities.

35
To experience new friends & positive emotions

Start making friends and being around others who are experiencing the feelings you want to experience. The most dangerous place for some of us is *alone* with our negative thoughts. Alone, and cut off from loved ones, is — for many of us — how the downward spiral of depression, loneliness and isolation begins. This is the wrong direction, and changing it requires being actively engaged and planning how you're going to find others to be around.

You may have to start by just going to a public place where people are around, going about their lives. When you get there, hold off comparing your life to theirs; avoid feeling lonely by sitting and being appreciative, and start to build hope of one day being able to experience the joy you see on some of their faces. This may be uncomfortable at first, but think of it as people-watching and research. You're looking for joyful or peaceful faces and connecting without saying a word.

Sometimes we've to see what joy or contentment looks like and build up a desire for it, before we can build it ourselves. I learned from many others by watching them before I built up the skill for myself. I watched speakers and trainers teach before I became one. Watching and learning from them showed me the basics, and I started to build a desire to do what they were doing — and to experience the same success in helping people have movements of discovery and revelation.

Step one: Be in places where there are people having fun, engaged in life, watching a concert, watching a street performer, sitting in a park. Be outdoors with people, not necessarily talking to them. You may feel awkward, but remember no one knows why you're there. You could be waiting for a friend, you could be reading a book, or you could be taking a break from work. People are concerned with themselves, not with you. Don't let thoughts of awkwardness cause you not to relax and enjoy the moment.

Step Two: Join a club, activity, or group where you're busy doing things with people, nothing risky or too intrusive. Join a group to learn a new skill: photography, art, car repair, crochet, golf, running. Choose something simple and enjoyable. You may feel anxious when you sign up or go to the first class or group, but it will feel good when you accomplish this first step and take a risk to change your life.

Step Three: Accept an invitation to an event — a night out, or something positive that allows other people to get to know you. The first two steps were safe and didn't allow others to get to know you more intimately. This step requires courage — but it can also bring the possibility of a new friendship, a great relationship, and rewards you may not have thought possible. Allow yourself to be known. You can have the fear — and still go ahead. "Courage is fear that has said its prayers."

36
Disappointment isn't defeat

You may have just been told:

"Sorry, we filled the position."

"This relationship isn't working out."

"You weren't the best-qualified candidate."

"The scholarships have been awarded and you didn't make the list."

"You weren't approved for the loan."

"We know you made extra payments, but we're still foreclosing on your house."

"I know you wanted to stay for another year, but the contract is being awarded to someone else."

"I have to take my business to another company. I know you just started this business."

Life will present many opportunities for you to find yourself feeling discouraged, disappointed, or defeated. In these moments it's important to experience the loss: maybe cry a tear, feel angry, or search for the reasons why this happened to you. Disappointment can leave you feeling cheated, perhaps thinking that someone else received what was rightfully yours. It can leave you feeling like the victim of cruel expectations because someone lied to you about your chances of success.

When we place our hope on one event or one person to make something happen, and it doesn't come to pass, we grieve, feeling the pain of loss.

Our hope may lead us to act as if the thing we want is already ours; we tell other people, as if it's a sure thing. We dream about it, imagine ourselves in that position or having the thing we've concentrated on, desired, and wished for. Some people will pray for it and believe that, yes, their faith will make it happen. These are all natural actions to take as we build expectation and hope.

But how do we deal with hope it when things don't' pan out ? By changing the way we look at what took place. We have a choice when facing disappointment, the opportunity to not let disappointment become defeat, and the choice to change how we see what's in front of us. You may have put all your hopes into one job opportunity or one client for your business, and this may have caused you to stop looking at other possibilities. After feeling the initial loss — the shock, the denial, the anger, the grief, the slowly dawning acceptance — let yourself take responsibility for the part you played, if any. Gently let yourself learn for next time. *When you lose, don't lose the lesson.*

37
Failure isn't the end; it's the beginning of the lesson

Failure isn't the end; it's the beginning of the lesson.
How will you know what the right answer is until you've
realized what the wrong one is? We've all failed — many
times! Some of us know the sting of failure big-time, where
the mistake was public or the consequence grave, and we
couldn't hide or blame someone else for it. In addition, we all
have had small failures in trying something new, or trying
time and again to break a harmful habit or overcome a
crippling life addiction.

Failure is a natural part of being human. Failure is the
result of trying and missing, of being too late or too early in
our timing. It's the result of saying something with innocent
intentions but being interpreted out of our intended context.
Perhaps, in retrospect, we took off running before we had all
the necessary information.

Failure can be the result of being blinded by our
arrogance or selfishness. Failure can happen when you're
trying to help someone, being selfless, but it wasn't needed —
or when the outcome wasn't what you planned. Then there
are times where something looks like a failure, but it creates
something new or brings a new possibility into your life.
That's why we need to see failure as an attempt — and to
give ourselves more chances. Most things that are worth
doing will take more than one try until we get them right.

Failure brings with it many opportunities to learn, or to try again or go in another direction. Failure doesn't mean you've come to the end of the road, because it may just be a fork in the road or a U-turn. It can also be a pause, a break, a chance to take the time to reevaluate and get the help of others to *think this through* before you try again. The important part of failure is what you become after you experience it — not what happens in the moment of failure itself. Failure can be a springboard for many other opportunities, a launching pad for your rocket of ideas. It can be a feeling that's experienced and transformed into fuel for your future success. *You* define what failure is going to mean in your life. You get to vote on how it's going to be written in the story of your life. Just because others have shared what they feel about your situation doesn't mean it's true! Their opinions shouldn't determine how you feel about what's happened.

If the failure was the result of an action or step taken:

Who says it's over?

Who said you couldn't win?

Is this the only way to achieve your goal?

What has the mistake taught you?

If given a chance to do it over, what would you do differently?

What's most important to you?

Why is this important?

If you could change something about your approach, what would you change?

116

Has this been done before? If so, how did other people do it? What could you add to or change about their method?

If the failure was because of something you said or did publicly:

What could you have said differently?

How can you make things right in a sincere and believable way?

How will you know something has changed?

What's it going to take to feel forgiven?

How do you make amends to the person or people you care about?

How can you prevent this from happening in the future?

How will you own your mistake and recover?

Have other people you know (or know of) committed a similar mistake? How did they recover?

What did you think of them, how did you express empathy toward them — and, if you didn't, how can you demonstrate empathy for them and for yourself now?

Choose to believe that next time you'll do it smarter, with more information, excited about the possibilities to learn and grow. Be determined that this goal is important to you. Don't give up because of failure, but instead use the lesson to learn and adjust. Be open to seeing things differently, to going about things in another way. There may be more than one approach to reach the ultimate goal you're striving for. Don't quit, don't give up, and don't let defeat get you down. Get up and move forward. Get up and try again from another angle, and with more information. You can win and you *will* win because of your change in thinking, your improved approach, and your being open to achieving the desired outcome in an unexpected and better way.

38
You deserve not to be judged by one moment of humiliation or a bad decision

Everyone has wanted to go back in time and erase or change something they said or did. Unfortunately, life doesn't allow us to go back and erase, but we can move forward and clean things up; we can move forward and pick up pieces and repair. Recovering from a mistake or a humiliating event is possible. You have to take ownership of the part you played in making it happen. Whatever was done to you — with or without your consent — that led to the embarrassment, rather than focusing on explaining or passing blame, stop and listen to those who were hurt by your actions. Acknowledge the damage that was done, and begin to figure out how you can help to make things better.

Scenarios that can be devasting:

Finding out you're the subject of an investigation which could lead to jail time

Getting arrested for driving under the influence and having your picture posted on a police website

Getting served divorce papers at work in front of coworkers

Having compromising photos or videos of you shared

Having your family find out you've been living a double life

Getting into a physical fight with a spouse or partner and being charged with domestic violence

A costly and long-term lawsuit being filed against you and your business

Being accused of sexual harassment, and having your family humiliated

Posting something on social media that's branded you a racist or sexist, causing the loss of your reputation and loss of significant amounts of money

These things may seem devasting at first, ending marriages and careers and ruining finances. However, it's important not to panic, and instead to respond slowly and deliberately. How fast you recover emotionally, as well as improving your reputation, will depend on your handling of the crisis or event. As long as you're living, you can recover. If you're not here — if your legacy ends with the event or scenario and taking of your life — then others are left to make up the story as to why you decided not to live anymore. Don't give the story or scenario over to others to decide; you choose the way it unfolds and how it turns around to benefit you.

This is done by staying in the fight to recover your reputation, and to change how others remember and experience you as a person. The event that took place should have a comma in between what happened and how you turned it around. You begin with a pause to assess the damage that's been done, and how big or small it is. Then you decide not to react, and instead to seek advice and plan how to recover slowly in a way that respects your rights and those of others. This isn't the time to explode with anger, or run around blaming or deflecting responsibility.

It will be difficult, and you'll have to repeat yourself, because things that are messy, salacious, or gossip-provoking are hard to quiet down and control.

Due to human beings' limited attention spans and the amount of new information coming to their minds on a daily basis, your situation will take a back seat in minds and leave their memories sooner than you think. Focus on the people who are directly impacted by what happened — the people who were hurt emotionally and financially, or physically affected by your decision or mistake. If they also suffered embarrassment or pain, then these are the people who won't forget easily, the ones you'll have to work at reaching out to in order to making amends.

Not caring, hiding, denying, or avoiding aren't solutions. They only prolong the pain and increase the level of humiliation and anger, or allow something that should have been a small matter to grow into a bigger issue. Take the situation and make something positive from it. Take a step back and acknowledge that everyone in their lifetime has faced a similar moment, maybe on a grander or smaller scale; but embarrassment, humiliation, being misunderstood, or making poor choices are simply part of the human experience.

Bouncing back, correcting, learning, and humbling ourselves are also part of the human experience. Just look at some public officials, actors, athletes, and entertainers who have bounced back from humiliating moments: Bill Clinton,

Robert Downey Jr., Brett Favre, Britney Spears, and many, many more.

Whether your moment or event was in the public eye or not, you can recover. Learn, grow, and help teach someone else not to make the same mistake or poor decision.

Move forward in small steps and start to repair what was broken with a sense of humility, You'll find there are kind people who understand and empathize, as well as some who may walk alongside you and help you rebuild your life and reputation. Depending on the nature of the event, it will take time, and always longer than you want, but it can turn around — and you can bounce back.

39
Life gets easier, and one day the opinions of others won't matter

Some things will take time because nothing else can change certain situations. Time to heal, time to let go, and time to forget, if necessary. It may feel like time can't move fast enough right now to put space between you and what's happened. Time can change things and heal relationships. The time factor helps you to look back when the feelings aren't as fresh, and to judge the situation from an older and hopefully wiser perspective.

Time isn't doing the actual healing, however; that work has to be completed in order to repair the emotional wounds. Time can't guarantee that you won't feel as angry or hurt when you see certain people again. Sometimes, just a picture on social media, or a familiar smell, or being in the area or home where something painful happened can bring back fresh emotions and memories that seem like yesterday. What time *can* do is allow you to have enough experience to help weigh against this experience. Time can help you build emotional strength and maturity to deal with a problem you couldn't deal with when you were younger or perhaps not as wise.

Time can help give you different perspectives, or even help you understand other people or circumstances more than you would have before. Time will give you the emotional and physical distance from the problem or issues, if you allow it.

When we're facing challenges, or when we're in emotional or physical pain, time seems to stand still. Time enables appreciation to take place and priorities to shift. For many of us when we're young our friendships are the most significant and most important relationships in our lives. In time, many of us get married and have children.

Marriages and children become the most important relationships in our lives. As we get older and start losing family members and kids grow up and out of the house, relationships with family members become more important again. Time changes are priorities, and we place new importance on the emotional value and weight we give each of our relationships. When you were younger, perhaps in high school, it may have been devastating when a friend stopped talking to you. Now, that you're older and have a family, that's not as painful and may not matter to you in the same way that it once did.

Time is a gift when you use it properly. Use time to get to learn more about yourself, and to gain distance from people or things that are harmful to your life. The time that can sees to pass so slowly will speed up and move much faster once you find something or someone who fills your interest again.

40

The pain will end, the tears will stop, and the darkness has to make way for the sun

Life gives us 24 hours a day, allowing us to live it in seconds, minutes, or hours. You get to choose how you experience it. Some days, we eat up the hours with television, the minutes with social media — and the day with worry. We choose how we spend the minutes and invest the hours; we decide whether to spend the time creating, or consuming.

What would happen if you decided to creat the life you want, rather than sit around, watching and worrying about the life you have?

Here's what may happen: little by little, each day would get easier. Therefore, every day, take small steps in moving forward and doing more. Start with a list of what you'd like to do if you felt better and stronger, and if the thing that's holding you back wasn't there anymore. Take this list and focus on *one thing*. Do something every day to get better than you are today and move closer to achieving the *one thing* on your list. Each step will build on the last one. Every new thing you accomplish will give you the added encouragement and energy to do the next thing.

There are times in life where we measure success and accomplishment in small increments. Until you feel stronger emotionally, let's work on building that muscle slowly, precisely, and deliberately by doing small things that will give you big rewards in the long run. Try to grow every day, just a little. For example, if yesterday you didn't get out of bed, today get out of bed. Tomorrow get out of bed and stay out all day, even if that means just moving to the couch. Then, the next day decide to get out the house for 15 minutes; then the next day 30, and the following day 1 hour. Movement is movement — and forward is still forward.

Take the small steps and just keep building. After every bit of progress and successful completion, congratulate yourself. Write it down, or record it on your phone. Give yourself credit right away, and each time do a little more. Joy comes from the small steps, continuously doing these things will change your habits over time. Your perspective and mindset will change as you see yourself taking action and reaching your goals. You'll find that your excuses grow less and less, and your enthusiasm grows more and more.

Start in small increments until going from 5 to 10 minutes of activity seems effortless, and soon you'll be up to 30 minutes — when before, that amount of time felt like an eternity. I don't like exercising. But when I tell myself, "Just get up and do a 10-minute workout video," then once my adrenaline is flowing and I'm warmed up I find myself doing two videos and slowly working up to 30 minutes. Now, a 10-minute video seems to too short — and since I'm already moving and sweating, I work out a little more, and end up feeling very accomplished and proud when I complete 30 minutes and elastic on the days I complete a 45-minute video.

This practice can be applied to any activity which you find yourself making excuses to avoid. Little by little, as you get more active, doing positive will improve your outlook and the days will get better. Take time to notice what's around you, and actively appreciate what brings you joy. Look around your home, your office space, or on your phone for the things that make you smile: a picture of someone you love, a gift you were given, a comfortable sweater, music you enjoy listening to. The pet that makes you smile, the sounds outside your window that remind you the world is active, and the people around.

Walk outside and notice what's changed from the day before. Feel the wind, listen to the sound of the rain, and experience the scent of the fog or the warmth of the sun. Remind yourself to appreciate the everyday, ordinary things around you — because that means the area you're in is stable, even if you feel your emotions aren't. Don't dread nighttime, because it means that tomorrow new opportunities are coming, and with them a chance to start over. Don't let the daytime waste away — because the minutes add up to hours of your life. Make it count by letting it feed your spirit. Make it count by being *awake and alert in the moment*. Make it work for you by intentionally doing something that will help you to grow and to feel better.

41

You're more than enough, and you're perfect in all your imperfection

There are things in nature that are beautiful and delicate — and once injured, they're changed forever. The change can alter their state but it doesn't have to change their purpose. Take, for example, a rose. When this beautiful, fragrant flower's petals fall, the state of the rose changes; it's not a complete rose, it's now a collection of petals. It can still be soft to the touch, and the color is beautiful; the smell can remain the same, or change as the flower begins to die or dry. The rose was perfect in its beauty, and as its shape changes, it isn't any less of a rose: it's just entered a different state of being. If the rose's petals are dried and kept in a vase, it's still a rose, but in a different state, and its purpose of being something beautiful and admirable hasn't changed.

The Leaning Tower of Pisa is a famous work of architecture that leans at a 10-degree angle. The tower has a 297-step spiral staircase inside, and it attracts thousands of visitors to the town of Pisa in Italy every year. This tower is imperfect, a big mistake when you measure it up against most other buildings. But people from all over the world travel to Italy to be amazed by its beauty — and find themselves laughing as they pose for pictures, pretending to hold up the tower. This mistake in the tower's planning hasn't made it less important or less beautiful. As a matter of fact, its imperfections have made it something more attractive and worth seeing.

Your imperfections are what make you unique. They don't take away from your worth as a human being. You're "fearfully and wonderfully made," according to the Bible. That means you've been made with precision, perfection, detail — and you're one-of-a-kind. Your imperfections aren't something to hate or hide, or to cause you shame. Imperfections are part of every human being.

If you're judging yourself by someone else's standard, ask yourself, "Is this fair to me? Is this fair to them, placing them on a pedestal?" Comparison is a practice that can leave you feeling jealous, robbed, intimidated, down, envious, sad, and ashamed. Don't put yourself on that emotional seesaw, where the other person is up and you're down.

You have everything you need in order to function. What we add to our lives are knowledge and experience. We change behavior and ways of thinking that are faulty. The fault isn't in our bodies or makeup, it's in our thinking, behavior, decisions, and choices, which are changeable.

You've been born with all you need; you are enough for the task and life ahead of you. In your imperfections, there are beauty, value, and potential. Strive for growth and development, not for perfection. You can live a full life and never know perfection because it's an impossible goal.

42
You'll get to call the shots

There are some people who are overbearing and manipulative to the point where you don't want to say anything around them. These are people for whom things are "their way or no way." You can find yourself getting lost in their shadows, or silenced by the volume of their voices. When they come into a room, the mood changes, people get quiet, and everyone has an emergency or starts to make an excuse to leave.

You may find yourself living or working with someone like this. If you're not careful, you can build resentment toward them and find yourself dreading interacting with them on a regular basis. This dynamic can change, and the feelings of dread can go away by enforcing boundaries.

To get your voice heard and begin to call the shots will require placing limits on others. You get to call the shots by telling others where your boundaries are. You decide what you will and won't do, letting others know what's allowed and what's unacceptable when it comes to being your friend, family member or coworker. You have the right to boundaries, and others have the right to respect your boundaries. If you've allowed someone to violate your boundaries, you may find yourself doing something that makes you uncomfortable. Be clear about what your limits are.

When it comes to relationships, boundaries at work, and with family and friends are necessary because they protect your rights and what's important to you.

Boundaries allow you to move comfortably in your relationships because you know what you will and won't allow. When people know what they can or can't do around you, then you have the freedom to relate to them with respect, and you feel a sense of safety because you know what to expect. Having boundaries gives you a healthy balance in how you relate to others. In a relationship without boundaries, one person's needs are getting met at the expense of another. Without healthy boundaries, one person could be doing things to please or hold on to a partner they're afraid of losing. Healthy boundaries allow you to acknowledge your feelings and needs, while allowing the other person to share how they can or can't help you to meet those needs. In addition, others ca share how they're experiencing or interpreting your actions.

Healthy boundaries allow each person in a relationship to show up as themselves. Your emotional and mental health and how you feel from moment to moment aren't tied to someone else. When there are no boundaries or healthy limits, one person's emotions are linked to another's. If mom is upset, everyone in the house is upset. If your husband or wife is sad or tired, then everyone is quiet and tiptoeing around them.

Unhealthy boundaries in couples sometimes looks like one person cheating and the other partner knowing and allowing it to continue out of fear of losing the person. If this situation is causing them emotional pain, and they're not

saying anything or asking for the respect they deserve from
their partner, there's a lack of boundaries in the relationship.

The partner who's not cheating isn't being valued in the relationship or expressing their needs for respect, accountability, and commitment to the relationship.

Unhealthy boundaries in relationships can look like a parent who calls and makes a demand of your time without verifying if it's okay to do so. The parent is blurring the lines with an adult child, treating them like a small child. This is the type of parent who tells you how to raise your own children, and argues or makes demeaning comments when you don't take their advice. In this type of relationship, when the child tries to do something differently or move away from the enmeshed parent, they're discouraged and given reasons why they'll fail if they leave home or move away.

Unhealthy boundaries with your ex-partner can leave you stuck, going back to past ways of communicating and interacting, and unable to move forward into a new relationship. If your ex is texting and calling, asking for favors after being separated or divorced, this is a sign that boundaries need to be set. The end of a relationship means the end of certain privileges with that person. If the connection is over and you're still meeting for sex, then something is wrong. If one of is thinking about reconciliation, while the other goes back to previous destructive behavior or harmful talk, then something is wrong. Either a boundary is being violated, or there are no established boundaries.

Destructive behaviors and relationships continue until someone starts to say "no" and sticks to their boundaries and limits.

Set rules on how the two of you are going to relate and communicate with each other. If you can't reach an agreement, it may not okay to be friends or continue the relationship. The leaving and coming back together when it's convenient, or when the other person is stressed or in need, is reactive and emotionally destructive.

Someone who loves and respects your boundaries will value your opinion and your desires. Therefore, when you say "no" it will be respected, and they won't try to manipulate you into changing your mind or bending to do things their way. They won't ask you to compromise your values, or live in a way that makes you feel guilty or ashamed. In healthy relationships with solid boundaries, you're free to express yourself. Your partner, friend, or parent is free to express themselves. Everyone feels honored and valued. You can have healthy and solid boundaries in relationships where your "yes" is affirmed and your "no" is respected.

43
You'll miss the best part

You'll miss the best part of the movie if you leave early. Think of your favorite movie: the beginning is just the foundation, laying the building blocks for everything that's to come. It doesn't always make sense in the beginning, but as you watch, it becomes clear. In the beginning, you learn about the characters. You learn about who you are at the beginning of your life, and as you grow, you discover what you do and don't like or agree with. You start with no control or ability to influence the outcome. Then, as you get older, you have more control, and you do have an impact.

But as life takes over, you face the good and the bad — and what may seem like the end is really just a subplot in your movie. It's not the end — or even the best part. If the devastation you're feeling is telling you this is the worst, and it won't get any better, that's *not* the truth. Where you are right now in your life may be the worst part yet, but you haven't experienced the *best* part of your life yet. The story of your life isn't over, and the best part is yet to come.

Your life began like a marathon, as you were surrounded by loved ones and many excited people who had been anticipating your birth. Much like runners at the beginning of the starting line, there are a lot of people ready to run the race with you, but the longer you run, the further you get from the starting line, the fewer people there are running with you.

139

If you pay attention to the signs, you may feel like getting off the path. You may look to find a path that seems shorter, as at some point your mind takes over.

You may ask yourself, "Why am I here?" "Why am I doing this?" And then, the big question comes: "Is this all worth it?" If you hang on to the end, you'll find out that it indeed is worth it. When you make it to the finish line, there will be another crowd waiting, people who are anticipating seeing you finish well. They will be the ones who remember you along the way. These are the helpers, coming to celebrate your life and your success.

44
You can live on the "right side" of your emotions

Negative emotions don't have to rule your thoughts or occupy space in your mind. You can tip the scales with conscious, continuous action, stopping the negative thoughts when they come into your mind and replacing them with positive thoughts. If you could see your thoughts outside your mind, they would be like words on a computer screen. As the negative words come across, pause and ask yourself, "Why am I thinking and feeling this way?" Then, replace the thought with the opposite positive thought.

Negative Thought:

"Life is unfair."

Change Thought:

"Life is sometimes unfair, but this won't stop me."

Negative Thought:

I should have worked harder to keep her in my life."

Change Thought:

"I can't control what someone else chooses to do. I can do my best and may have to make changes, but the decision is still up to them."

Negative Thought:

"I got fired from my job; I'm a failure."

Change Thought:

"Getting fired doesn't mean I'm a failure. I'll learn from this experience, and I'll get another job."

Negative Thought:

" I'll never love anyone as I loved my spouse."

Change Thought:

"I'll fall in love again, and the next relationship will be different. I don't have to love the next person the same to have a great relationship."

Negative Thought:

"No one will ever want me after this."

Change Thought:

" I'm loveable, and the right person will come into my life at the right time."

Practice stopping the negative thoughts and asking: "Why this thought, and why now?" This will help you understand how your thoughts and your emotions are connected. Asking yourself what you saw, heard, or felt before the thought came into your mind will help you link the thought to a trigger. The trigger is something that happened to get your mind thinking negatively.

After stopping and recognizing the thought, practice replacing it with a positive — or even a neutral — thought. A neutral thought, for example, would be, "I didn't get the job, but it's okay." This thought is neutralizing negative feelings, not necessarily building positive ones. (And that's okay.)

Another practice that helps to sort out negative emotions and learn how to eliminate or diminish them is to identify what you're feeling. This happens most often with the emotion of anger. Anger is the response, but the real emotion

142

could be pain, fear, loss, shame, humiliation, uncertainty, sandess, or other feelings.

Knowing and acknowledging what you're feeling — and why — can help you to address the issue and change it.

Take the list below and use it as a starting point to get on the right side of your emotions.

Negative	Positive
Sad	Happy
Doubtful	Certain
Envious	Content
Shameful	Proud
Hateful	Empathetic
Fearful	Hopeful
Anxious	Calm
Angry	Joyful

If you often find yourself having one or more of these negative emotions during the day, this may be a clue to the feeling and issue you want to explore first in counseling. If there's a negative emotion you're feeling frequently during the day, set a goal to feel the corresponding positive emotion by stopping and replacing the thought that led to the feeling.

Remember your feelings aren't always the truth about what's going on. Feelings can be misinterpreted. You can create a different feeling, change your awareness, and change how you interpret your experiences. You're creating your daily mindset by the emotions you choose to hold on to, and your responses to them. What you choose to focus on shapes your life.

45
You deserve to make decisions you're proud of

Don't make a decision when you're hungry, alone, tired, angry or lonely. These are the four worst times emotionally or mentally to make any decisions. If you've ever shopped in the supermarket when you were hungry, I'm sure by the time you left the supermarket you'd purchased more food than you intended to, and perhaps nothing on your original list. This is why it's an excellent idea to eat before you go food shopping. This way, you're full and not easily tempted to buy more food than you need. When you're physically hungry, your mind and mental resources focus on getting food into your body for survival, and your ability to make good decisions decreases because the desire to eat quickly takes over.

Why is it a good idea not to make decisions when you're alone? When you're alone, you're not capable of seeing and taking into consideration other points of view. This is because when you're by yourself, you can't always obtain accurate information before making choices. When alone, we think our thoughts are valid and correct since we have no one to debate with, or bounce our thoughts off of. Although you may be tempted to believe that your opinion is the best, and everyone or anyone you talk to would understand why you made a choice you've made, sadly, that's not necessarily true. Until you share with others what you're going through, then the best decision isn't the one in your mind — because you don't know.

You need someone else to challenge your thinking before you make the biggest mistake of your life. Give yourself that chance and give the testing of your thinking and theories a chance.

Have you ever been so tired that you fell asleep while thinking — or felt so sleepy that others would think you were drinking just by the way you walked or talked? Fatigue can cause brain fog that stops you from thinking clearly. Sleep deprivation has been used as a form of torture because it works. You're not thinking straight after no sleep, or just one to two hours' worth of sleep. Some studies have equated the effects of lack of sleep to being under the influence of toxic substances. If you're sleepy, frustrated, and uncertain, don't make any decisions. Get help finding regular, quality sleep, and you'll see improvements in your mood, your thinking, and your health.

Loneliness causes us to make poor decisions, for instance in choosing a partner, or having one-night fling. Loneliness and the desperation to have someone love us has led men and women to build online relationships that leave them broke, betrayed, and suffering unintended consequences. Everyone has a need to be loved, and to feel a sense of purpose, approval and validation by others. When those needs aren't being met, we'll do whatever it takes to get a need met — even if it means doing it illegitimately. The legitimate need for affection may lead to paying for a prostitute, which can bring legal trouble and worse into your life.

Making decisions when mentally, emotionally, or physically not at your best is a recipe for disaster and regret. Wait till you're stronger in all those areas before making any final decisions. Take your time; get fit emotionally, physically, and financially. Take time to see things and people from a different perspective, and to allow hope to build.

46
Nothing — I mean *nothing* — stays the same forever; if you keep on living, things will change

Everything has a season. Sports have seasons, the weather changes with the season, humans have seasons in their lives. The beauty of life is that nothing human or animal ever stays the same. We all move through time, grow, and develop, whether we want to or not. Time causes human to become older and animals to live out their lifespans.

The choice lies in fighting the growth — or in growing with the changes in the seasons of your life. Human beings are born to grow and evolve, from a child to an adult. When we don't grow physically or mentally, this is an indicator that something is wrong. When we aren't growing and developing, we feel frustrated. This restlessness is a sign that it's time to change, move, or do something different.

Sometimes, you're in a comfortable place and you don't want to leave it because it's easy and familiar. Familiar isn't always healthy or the best for us, however, because it doesn't always align with our goals. Ordinary can be a trap when it doesn't allow or motivate you to grow and positively challenge yourself. When you're 14 years old and playing video games, it's a season. But when you're 40, unless you're a professional gamer, playing video games for long periods of time seems unnatural, and a stunt in growth. Things are meant to change in order for human beings to grow in knowledge and progress.

Keep on living because things *will* change — and when they do, grab hold and take advantage of it. The problem you're facing today may seem insurmountable, impossible, or life-altering. Give it time; something in the scenario will change as you receive more information and clarity.

With the change in seasons, you'll find things that were once hard now come easily. What seemed at one time impossible and out of reach will fall into your lap, and you'll walk right through. Where once it felt like you stood under the pressure of a certain problem or issus, now you'll walk over it, like a bridge, to the next phase in your life.

47

You control how many letters in the alphabet you want to use: Plan A, B, C, D

If your plan A for changing your life didn't work, it's not over. Make a plan B, C, and D. Keep trying until you find the one that works. Right now, life has you feeling as if there are no other options. Don't let your feelings lie to you. Don't let the narrow focus of your mind *at this moment* confuse or limit your thinking. There are other options.

There are other ways and plans that will work to improve your life. You have to give yourself time and the chance to discover the different options that are available to you. There are other options in the dating and marriage side of life; your ex-wasn't the only option for being happy with a partner. You can and will find another partner with whom to share life experiences. According to the world population clock, there are 8 billion people on the planet. Your ex-partner was just one of 8 billion people in the world; it's certain that you have other options to start a new relationship.

Take the job you lost: according to the Bureau of Labor and Statistics, that job was one out of ten jobs you'll hold during *half* of your life. You still have the other half of your life to have ten more jobs — or several more careers. That job you lost may seem like it was the best one, or a dream job — until you find your next career, and then you'll look back and ask yourself, "Why was I so worried?" There are more jobs in different places and more opportunities to explore all of your talents.

Stick around. Don't quit five minutes before the miracle.

If you've lost a loved one and are in the stages of grief, all the previous examples will seem trivial. When dealing with loss, this isn't about replacement but about building: building on the legacy and creating more from the memories and contributions of your loved ones. No one is perfect, but everyone has something to teach us, and if we're willing to hear and apply it, we can grow emotionally and spiritually as the result of a loved one passing away.

There are times where we don't replace, but we *rebuild* on a foundation that was already chosen and prepared for us. When the plan that you had stopps working for you, make a new plan, and set new goals. Your recovery will be slow, but you'll improve. Find a plan that works, or let the plan set a new life in motion for yourself. Don't cut it short, because *the best is yet to come*. The best part of your life is in front of you, so *hold on* and get through this time.

48
Your creator is incredibly in love with you, no matter how you feel about yourself

We can't address the issue or thoughts of suicide without addressing the spiritual part of your makeup. You're a multifaceted being with a body, mind, and spirit. Your connection to your creator right now may be loose or tenuous, but if you're considering something so final as suicide, consider instead entering into seeking and knowing the relationship with the God who created you.

Energy, strength, confidence, peace, and a sense of purpose can come from learning and knowing that you're not here by accident or luck. You're here for a purpose, designed uniquely for you. The God of the universe was deliberate in creating you with everything you'd need for survival and to thrive.

In you, there's beauty, creativity, joy, hope, and the blueprint for building a legacy for your family and your children, if you have them. Your life is meant to declare the beauty and majestic nature of your creator. Your life has value; you were created to live out your gifts, your talents, and your contribution to the world. Everyone and everything plays a part in what we know as the beauty of life. What makes the world beautiful is the way each person, animal, and every living organism plays its part in the beauty of life.

We may take for granted the trees, rain, dogs, cats, and birds, being able to enjoy the air or the landscape because of the beautiful plants, animals, and trees around us. We can smile and laugh, watching dogs and cats being silly on video or in real life as we walk down the street. There's a sound, feeling, and beauty in how life flows and connects with itself. You're a part of this beautiful and complicated existence, sometimes painful and magnificent all at once.

Your life is meant to demonstrate the beauty and magnificence of your creator. When life is hitting you with everything it has, and your mind feels trapped in the spiral or wheel of negative thoughts, explore all of who you are and use every tool available for conquering depression, anxiety, and uncertainty. Explore mental health, and look for physical and spiritual tools to help you win against depression. The God of the universe is incredibly in love with you, desires to hear you, and wants to take your pain and help you experience a love and peace that's achieved through a spiritual relationship with the world around you.

49
You'll miss the chance to get clear, feel whole, and live pain-free

When the pain of what you're going through becomes a combination of physical and emotional distress, you can easily find yourself drifting with thoughts of going to sleep and not getting back up, and wanting to escape the pain because it's overwhelming. If you can't see how to manage the pain, and the moments of intensity are becoming more and more frequent, suicide can seem like a way out. But the thought of a quick fix for the uncertain problem and unknown timeline of when it's going to end isn't the way out.

Sleeping your pain away isn't a solution. Ending your life isn't a solution, because it will pass on your pain to the ones you love. It's not a solution because you cannot guarantee that other lives won't be lost in your attempt. It's not a solution because if you attempt and live, there may be some very tragic, painful, and more devasting consequences.

Scaries of all, perhaps, is that you don't even know if the pain *will* end.

It has been said that the fastest way to get over or past something is to go through it — not to go around, escape, or run. Go through the temporary pain in order to survive and live pain-free, whole, healthy and peaceful.

The negative thoughts are crippling because they trigger limited feelings, which can change. You can get help to alleviate the physical pain and symptoms. You can get counseling and medication to help you with the depression and other feelings.

So, if your mind is telling you that suicide is the only option, it's wrong. There are many other options, possibilities that are full of hope, and a new life after this. You can heal through this time, you can change, and the pain can decrease and eventually disappear altogether.

If you think you're a burden to others because you have been sad or depressed for a long time, if you've dealt with chronic pain or illness and are thinking your loved ones would be better without you, this is *not* true. *You are not a burden.* If the choice is to have you in their lives and sharing memories together, or not having you in their lives, your family will always choose to have you despite the challenges of your pain or illness. This is what love does. Love is willing to be convinced, willing to give and, if necessary, to sacrifice and do more so the family can thrive and survive. It's not selfish of you to want to live and not rely on others; give your loved ones a chance to experience this time with you.

Don't isolate yourself from the people who love you. You're connected to them, and they to you. Enjoy and grow the connection by not removing them from your life. Answer the phone, go outside and say "yes" to times and events where you can get connected and make memories.

Reach out. Choose life. You have an option where no one gets hurt, where you're not committing a crime to get relief. The people you love and who love you can help — if you're open to sharing with them. Don't make a mistake or decision that will bring so much pain to your family, friends, and community by taking your life. Your life has value, you are needed, and things *will* get better.

50
To experience putting down the mask

If you live your life in the public eye, it's increasingly difficult to have a separate private and public life because the two worlds frequently mix. As much as you may try, how you carry on your life privately will be known publicly in time. Therefore, how do you manage and live freely, be authentic and congruent? It's a process to feel comfortable and confident, to live authentically. The benefit of living authentically is the freedom from fear and the anxiety that comes from living a life of duplicity.

Becoming authentic means allowing your personality and moral character to be in harmony. This helps you when you face external forces that pressure you to do things and become someone who you're not. When the real you comes through, people either accept it or move toward someone who they feel more connected to.

If you need the applause, approval, and attention of others, sadness and doubt will seep into your mind and heart when you don't receive it. The addiction to approval or applause is a sign of needs that aren't being met. It also indicates an area that needs healing. Seeking approval and accolades is like chasing a butterfly: no sooner do you have it in your hand than with a small opening of the palm, it's gone again. You gain pleasure for a moment, proud of your accomplishment, and then you're back to chasing the feeling and the experience again.

To stop the chase and take off the mask of an image, start with getting honest, with matching your beliefs and behaviors. Once this work has begun, you feel greater peace because the guilt, shame, and worry that someone will find out you're not who you pretend to be will fade. There will be the freedom of not having to worry, not wondering, "Will they find out I'm not really smart, I don't know what I'm doing, I don't belong here?" You'll have the freedom to move and live in the world according to your personality and quirks, and by supporters with love. You can live free of the mask. It will take time, but the work is worth it — and being a public figure doesn't exclude you from this freedom.

51

Don't make an irreversible decision based on a situation that's subject to change

Hope alone may not feel like it's enough, but we have to decide to move forward. I want you to plan your next step by making a firm decision. Plan for how you're going to live — because hope is fragile, and has to be anchored in something.

Circumstances can conceal hope, and doubt can take it away. It can be taken away by listening to the words of someone else that are given too much weight. A sense of helplessness can make hope difficult to imagine or believe. When despair seems hard to overcome, you to have nurture hope and look for ways to rebuild and keep going.

Start by getting a piece of paper, or the phone, and create your reason-to-live list. Write the small and significant reasons you want to live — even the reasons why the people in your life, family, friends, and community want you to live. Part two of this activity is to list what you're going to try in the future. What do you need to make new, hopeful activity happen? Who in your life can help you to get it done? Write down what you plan on doing if discouragement sneaks up on you again, and list people to whom you can talk.

I also want you to plan on how you're going to be safe if you have more thoughts about suicide. Save the phone number for the Suicide Prevention Lifeline: (800) 273-8255 (that's 800-273-TALK). If you're outside the United States, please research the helpline or center for your area.

Have the phone number in your wallet, and program the number into your phone or download one of the suicide prevention applications to help you find resources.

Start the search to find a therapist in your area. If you can't afford a therapist, find a support group in your area. Consider finding a local church or synagogue to gain spiritual support.

Have a safe space you can go to when you need time to think. This safe place should be somewhere that you're *not* entirely alone. The safe place should be in the vicinity of people, and it should allow you to have some quiet — for example, a local park. Find a little space to sit and think. A safe space can be a local library, a museum or art gallery, someplace that will help you get quiet where you won't be alone.

You don't want to be any place where you can harm yourself, or others. Most importantly, if you have no other option and you're feeling like you don't want to go on, please go to your nearest emergency room and get help.

Make a plan for how you're going to get help, or how to connect with others if you're having negative thoughts about living. Call someone — and try *more than one* person, because there's a chance the first person could be tied up in a work meeting, or their phone could be off, or the battery is out of power. The first person could be asleep, or perhaps they forgot their phone at home that day.

When you're in trouble or feeling discouraged, have several people that you can reach out and talk to. If needed, go outside your house! Go knock on the neighbor's door and talk to your neighbor. If you're considering something so final as to take your life, *don't let fear stop you* from reaching out to *anyone or everyone* for the help. Give yourself a fighting chance. You deserve a fighting chance! Give yourself one more chance. One more day, and one more try.

Give yourself an opportunity to prove yourself wrong, to prove your thinking wrong. Give the people around you a chance to help you. When you need help, don't let pride or fear of others knowing your business stop you from getting help.

Suicide leaves everyone who loves you feeling robbed, hurt, and upset. They could end up blaming themselves, feeling they weren't able to be there for you to help you when you needed it most. Give your loved ones the chance to show you that they care, and will be there for you. Your loved ones genuinely love you. Share with them the truth about your despair and your sense of hopelessness.

Suicide is an excruciating choice. It's painful for the person who's considering it, and devastating for all the people left behind with no answers. Also, there will be unanswered questions and emotional pain; their lives are robbed of yheir relationship with you.

Suicide takes family, loved ones, and anybody connected to their loved one into heavy grief, so devastating that it will take years to recover well. Some people don't heal well, and a

162

terrible new hardship is now in their lives. Their loss is tremendous.

The people left behind may not understand their loved one's decision to end their life was a misguided attempt to feel better, forget, or disappear. This choice can inflict pain that's indescribable, personal, and devastatingly traumatic for the people we love the most. Think about them, and the kind of sadness and heartbreaking loss that they're going to feel because of losing you. Without you alive, they will feel deprived of a lifetime of knowing you, connecting and building memories.

If they lose you, it will change their lives forever. Consider what everybody else has to lose and what you'll lose if you make this decision. Give yourself a fighting chance; get the help you need.

Make the phone call, get to the therapist's office, go to the hospital, knock on the neighbor's door to get help today, *right now*. Make a plan for living, decide on how you're going to get your peace back, one step at a time. You can win over those negative thoughts. Walk out of the darkness, make a plan that says, "I'm worth living for, and just for today I'll live, I'll give myself one more day, one more week and one more year to reach my goals to take control of my life."

52
Your Life Matters

Your life matters and your best years, best ideas, and best memories are in front of you — *not* behind you.

Here are **little and big ways your life matters:**

You made someone laugh

You helped someone get up after a fall

You said something encouraging to another human being

You stopped and gave someone a spot, a chance, a gift

You helped someone see danger ahead

You called at the right time when a friend was down

You stopped by the house of someone who was feeling down, and spent time with them

You were at a birthday party, becoming a part of someone's memories

You gave someone money to help them accomplish what they couldn't do on their own

You shared your lunch, dinner, or snack

You stood up for something by joining a group, signing a petition, or sharing a social media post

You showed up to work and did a good job

You served others at work or at home

You took care of someone who needed help

You loved another human being

You expressed appreciation to a parent or family member

You didn't share someone's personal information, and helped protect them from feeling shame

You hugged someone at the right time

You gave up your time to help someone in need

You defended someone who couldn't protect themselves

You exposed a lie

You told the truth — even though it was difficult

You stopped doing something that was harmful to others

You shared something personal, allowing someone to be vulnerable in front of you

You helped improve a garden, yard, or playground

You spent time with a lonely person who felt like an outcast

You said "thank you" to someone who felt unappreciated

You loved the unlovable

You remembered an important day in someone else's life

You showed compassion to someone who was hurt

You protected someone from public embarrassment

You had the heart to reach out and help a friend when others gave up them

You helped someone learn how to do something new

You did something for someone else, expecting nothing in return

You gave up something you liked so that someone else could have something they needed

In more ways than you can know, you're important, and your life is valuable. My hope is that one or more of the reasons listed above have helped you to remember and discover possibilities and hope for your future.

This is just the beginning. Continue to grow your hope, and to heal by getting the care and support your need to realize your potential and to have peace in your mind.

Resources:

National Suicide Prevention Lifeline: 1-800-273-8255

The Lifeline provides 24/7, free and confidential support for people in distress, prevention and crisis resources for you or your loved ones, and best practices for professionals.

The Veterans Crisis Line connects veterans in crisis and their families and friends with qualified, caring Department of Veterans Affairs responders. Veterans and their loved ones can call 1-800-273-8255 and press 1, chat online, or send a text message to 838255 to receive confidential support 24 hours a day, 7 days a week, 365 days a year.

SAMHSA Treatment Referral Hotline (Substance Abuse):
1-800-662-HELP (4357)

RAINN National Sexual Assault Hotline:
1-800-656-HOPE (4673)

National Teen Dating Abuse Helpline
1-866-331-9474

If you suspect a friend or loved one is thinking about suicide, don't hesitate to ask directly if they're having thoughts of committing suicide. **Don't make assumptions.** Listen, show compassion, and let them know you care, while getting them connected to treatment. Call the National

Suicide Prevention lifeline at 1-800-273-8255 to get them connected to a therapist or doctor in their area. Avoid giving your opinions and advice on the topic because this can be debated or viewed as minimizing their problems, focus on the reasons to live and getting them to the support services needed.

www.ingramcontent.com/pod-product-compliance
Lightning Source LLC
Chambersburg PA
CBHW060038040426
42331CB00032B/1013